Introduction Ireland

A Quick Travel Guide for Ireland in 2019

© Copyright 2019 - All rights reserved.

The content contained within this book may not be reproduced, duplicated or transmitted without direct written permission from the author or the publisher.

Under no circumstances will any blame or legal responsibility be held against the publisher, or author, for any damages, reparation, or monetary loss due to the information contained within this book. Either directly or indirectly.

Legal Notice:

This book is copyright protected. This book is only for personal use. You cannot amend, distribute, sell, use, quote or paraphrase any part, or the content within this book, without the consent of the author or publisher.

Disclaimer Notice:

Please note the information contained within this document is for educational and entertainment purposes only. All effort has been executed to present accurate, up to date, and reliable, complete information. No warranties of any kind are declared or implied. Readers acknowledge that the author is not engaging in the rendering of legal, financial, medical or professional advice. The content within this book has been derived from various sources. Please consult a licensed professional before attempting any techniques outlined in this book.

By reading this document, the reader agrees that under no circumstances is the author responsible for any losses, direct or indirect, which are incurred as a result of the use of information contained within this document, including, but not limited to, — errors, omissions, or inaccuracies.

ISBN: 9781092539234

Table of Contents

Table of Contents..3
Introduction...8
Chapter 1: A Brief History of Ireland.................10
Chapter 2: Ireland Today...................................11

State of Government and Politics............................11
Government..11
Politics..11

Population..12

Culture...12
St. Patrick's Day...13
Irish Dancing...13
Irish Music..14
Legends and Myths of Ireland......................................14

Sports/Recreation.......................................15
Soccer...15
Horse Racing...15
Rugby...15
Gaelic Games..16

Chapter 3: Why You Should Go To Ireland........17

Ireland Has Amazing Castles.....................17
Dublin, the crown Jewel of Ireland..........18
Don't Forget About Irish Folklore............19
Everyone Should Have An Irish Adventure...........20
There is No Scenery Like Irish Scenery..................20
Two Words: Irish Food...............................21
No Matter Where You Look, You'll Find History....22

You Can Experience Pub Culture..........................22

There is a Guinness Storehouse........................23

Makes for Easy Travel All the Way Round.............24

Ireland is Home to the Wild Atlantic Way.............24

Giant's Causeway..25

The Irish are Very Friendly..................................26

Chapter 4: Best Time To Go.............................27

Ireland Month By Month.....................................28
January..28
February..28
March..29
April..29
May..30
June...30
July..31
August...31
September...31
October..32
November..32
December...33

Shoulder Season...33

Chapter 5: Weather Throughout The Year........34

The Perfect Time To Visit...................................34

The Weather of the Seasons..............................35

The Key is the Wardrobe...................................35

Tackle Ireland's Weather With These Tips..........36

Chapter 6: Estimated Costs of Your Trip...........37

Estimated Cost for One Person..........................37
Estimated Cost for A Couple or Family....................38

Travel Costs Explained......................................38
Accommodations...38

 Airfare..39
 Transportation..40
 Food..40
 Attractions..41
 Extras..41

Chapter 7: What To Pack....................................43

The Necessities..43

Personal Items..44

Packing for Adventurous Weather.......................45

Packing Your Technology....................................45

Clothing..46

Anything Extra?...46

What You Should Not Bring...............................47

 Items of Sentimental Value..47
 Camouflage Clothing...48
 Heavy Items...48
 Expensive Items..48
 Fanny Packs...48

Chapter 8: Methods of Travel...............................49

Air Travel..49

Ferry...49

 Holyhead to Dublin Ferry..50
 Liverpool to Dublin Ferry..50
 Liverpool Birkenhead to Belfast Ferry.................................50
 Roscoff to Cork Ferry..50
 Cairnryan to Larne Ferry..51
 Santander to Cork Ferry...51

Take a Cruise..51

 European Classic Cruise to Ireland.....................................51
 Amsterdam to Dublin...52
 Ireland, Scotland, and Cornwall...52

Chapter 9: Currency in Ireland.............................53

Does all of Ireland use the same currency............53

Can I use American Dollars In Ireland...................54

Can I use debit and credit cards in Ireland............54

BONUS: List of Great Currency Apps.....................55
My Currency Converter..55
Travel Calculator...55
All Currency Converter..55
XE Currency..55
Currency Convert..56
Currency Pro...56
Easy Currency Converter...56
X Convert...56
Amount..56

Chapter 10: Places to Visit............................58

Muckross House, Gardens, and Killarney National Park..58

Dublin..59

Galway...60

Limerick..60

Kilkenny..61

Cork...62
Elizabeth Fort..62
St Fin Barre's Cathedral..62
University College Cork..63
Cork Butter Museum...63
Cork City Gaol..63

Aran Islands..64

Antrim, Northern Ireland..................................64
2019 Open Championship will be held here............................64
Ballintoy Harbour filming location for Iron Islands in "Game of Thrones."...64
Giant's Causeway 65
Dunluce Castle..65

Carrickfergus Castle..66
Landscapes..66
Glens of Antrim...66

Chapter 11: Tours You Should Go On.................68

Best of Ireland Tour..68
Day 1: Dublin to Kilkenny...68
Day 2: Kilkenny to Kinsale, County Cork..................................69
Day 3: Kinsale to Killarney..69
Day 4: Killarney, the Ring of Kerry, and Muckross House..........69
Day 5: Killarney to Galway...70
Day 6: Galway and the Connemara Region................................70
Day 7: Galway to Dublin...71
Day 8: Dublin and its Many Sights to See..................................71
Day 9: End of Your Tour...72

Cliffs of Moher Tour..72

Game of Thrones Tours..72

Cork Ghost Tour..73

Castle Tours..73
Trim Castle..73
Ross Castle...74
Dublin Castle...74

Malahide Castle..74

Pub Tours..74
Rural Pub Tours..75
Connemara Pub Tours..75
Irish Pub Tour...75
Dublin Traditional Irish Music Pub Crawl................................76

Chapter 12: Attractions to Behold......................77

Cliffs of Moher..77

Ring of Kerry..78

Rock of Cashel..78

Guinness Storehouse..79

    Dunluce Castle...79
Chapter 13: Safety in Ireland.............................80
    Medication..80
    Emergency Numbers...80
    Crime in Ireland..81
    Bag snatchers and Pickpocketers...........................82
    Sexual Assault or Robbery......................................83
    Credit Card, Fraud, and Scams...............................84
Conclusion..86
Bonus Chapter: Little Known Irish Facts..........87
Bibliography...90

Introduction

When we travel, we are always looking for the next interesting and fun adventure. Sometimes, we choose destinations based on family history. We want to go back to the homeland of our ancestors to find out where they really came from and what their lives were like in the past. Other times, we decide on a destination because of history. We might have learned about a country's history, making us invested in the location. And other times, we just want to go to a place to learn more about the culture and see as many things as possible.

For all the above reasons, one of the most popular tourist destinations is Ireland. Known for the luck of the Irish, St. Patrick's Day, leprechauns, and the color green, Ireland holds so much more history, beauty, and amazing sights to see than people realize. If you're thinking about checking out Ireland in your next major vacation, this travel guide is for you.

In this book, I will discuss a brief history of Ireland, but will also talk about what to expect in Ireland today. I will discuss the state of politics and the government, culture, population, sports, and recreation. I will talk about the weather in Ireland, as well as the best times to travel. I will discuss why to choose Ireland and the type of costs associated with it. I will help you with your packing, inform you about Ireland's currency, methods of travel, and places to visit. I will also take time to discuss safety in

Ireland. And, if you keep reading until the end of the book, there will be a little special fun bonus for you!

Recently, Tripadvisor named Ireland as the second best place to visit in the world. In total, 194 other countries were up for the award, and the only country to beat Ireland was Iceland. These awards came from Tripadvisor's annual international awards, which ranks the best vacation spots. How could you not want to visit Ireland when it has ranked second in Tripadvisor's list on one of the best places to visit in the world? In fact, no matter what information I put in this travel guide, there is still so much more you can see in Ireland. I would need to write a dozen travel guides in order to give you the right amount of information that you can see in Ireland. With all the tourist attractions, friendly Irish citizens, and so much more, it should come as no surprise that when people visit Ireland once, they return!

Recently, Tripadvisor named Ireland as the second best place to visit in the world. In total, 194 other countries were up for the award, and the only country to beat Ireland was Iceland. These awards came from Tripadvisor's annual international awards, which ranks the best vacation spots. How could you not want to visit Ireland when it has ranked second in Tripadvisor's list on one of the best places to visit in the world? As I have already said, there is an abundance of things to do and see in Ireland! I would need to write a dozen travel guides in order to give you the right amount of information that you can see in Ireland. With all the tourist attractions, friendly Irish citizens, and so much more, it should come as no surprise that when people visit Ireland once, they return!

Chapter 1:

A Brief History of Ireland

For any tourist, one of the best features of Ireland is its long history. Like many other countries, Ireland has a rich history, but it's also one of the few countries where you are able to see buildings and sites from centuries ago. For example, when you visit Ireland, you'll most likely find a prehistoric tomb or castles from the 17th or 18th century. Also, as you travel through Ireland, you'll get a taste of Irish folklore. All of this shows Ireland's rich history, so you won't want to miss that in your journey.

It's believed that people first stood on what is now Irish territory around 8,000 to 4,000 B.C. For thousands of years, groups of people came and went through Ireland, with some groups staying longer than others. Around 500 B.C., the Celts came to Ireland and since then, the culture has become known as the Irish culture.

One of the most significant events of Ireland's history is the return of Saint Patrick, who is believed to have come back in 432 A.D. Since then, Ireland has had a rich history with the Christian religion. Ireland's history kept growing, and in 795 A.D., the Scandinavian Vikings stepped foot on Irish soil.

Like nearly every other country in the history of the world, Ireland could not escape wars and disasters. However, as you can see, none of this takes away from the beauty of Ireland today. In fact, all the events in Ireland's history helped it grow into what it's known as today. One of the best ways to discuss the history of Ireland is by reading this travel guide. Throughout the chapters of this travel guide, you will read about attractions that date back to thousands of centuries ago. On top of this, the most amazing way to learn about Irish history is by taking a trip to Ireland. While in this guide, I will discuss Irish history a little, there is really nothing like being up close and personal with its history, especially when it's a castle from the 12th or 13th centuries!

When you take your vacation to the fabulous island of Ireland, you will run into so much Irish history. It seems that nearly every attraction within Ireland, from the castles to the pubs to the Cliffs of Moher, is oozing with loads of rich history. As knowledgeable as they are, the guides you meet during your tours probably won't even be able to tell you every bit of history the attraction you're viewing holds. Just think about it - some castles and pubs were easily built hundreds of years ago. How could anyone know the whole history of such a majestic location? Especially one as wondrous as Ireland! There are dozens of reasons for people to visit the Emerald Isle. It's rich and remarkably preserved history is just one of them.

Chapter 2:

Ireland Today

While the history of your next destination is always fun to learn, you must also understand the country's current state. In this chapter, we will look at Ireland's government and its political state. We will also discuss Irish culture and its population so that you're a little more aware of what to expect when you arrive. At the end of this chapter, we will also discuss sports and recreation in Ireland.

State of Government and Politics

Government

The Taoiseach is the Prime Minister, and he is the head of the government in Ireland. Underneath him is the Deputy Prime Minister, the Tánaiste. From there, various ministers help run the government. Together, these people hold the executive power of Ireland under the Constitution. Ireland's government is a parliamentary democracy, with a total of 15 governmental departments.

The Oireachtas is known as the Parliament of Ireland, and Dáil Éireann and Seanad Éireann are the two Houses of Parliament. There are about 166 members in the Dáil

Éireann and around 60 in the Seanad Éireann. When it comes to the Oireachtas, it runs similar to the United States government. The Dáil Éireann is basically the House of Representatives, and the Seanad Éireann is the Senate.

Michael D Higgins is the President of Ireland. Each president has a term of around seven years and they can be re-elected, but cannot serve more than a couple of terms.

As the government of Ireland trickles down, you will find about 114 local authorities with various jobs, like housing, waste management, health, welfare, transportation, education, and water supply.

Politics

Ireland has four main political parties. These include the Fine Gael, Labour, Sinn Fein, and Fianna Fail. On top of this, there are politicians in Ireland who are not a part of a particular party, as well as many smaller parties that aren't as popular. Today, the government is mainly run under two of the four main parties, which are the Labour and Fine Gael parties.

Population

In 2018, Ireland was home to 4,803,748 people. This number went up from the previous year, as in 2017, it had a population of 4,761,657. In fact, Ireland's population has been dramatically increasing for decades. In 1955, Ireland's population was 2,899,784. Its population then decreased for a couple of years, but not by much. In 1975, it jumped to 3,184,126, and it has continued to increase ever since.

Culture

Ireland has a very fun and unique culture that everyone needs to not only learn about, but actually experience for themselves!

Many of the holidays celebrated all over the world started in Ireland, and I'm not just talking about St. Patrick's Day. Halloween also started in Ireland, before moving to many other places around the world. Halloween came to the United States from Irish Immigrants who brought their culture to North America. Originally, in Ireland, Halloween was known as Samhain and considered a Celtic Festival.

The Irish Language is called the Celtic language, and there are two main languages in Ireland today, Irish and English.

The Irish are very proud of their food and drink. Of course, meat is some of their favorite food, as well as potatoes, cereal, vegetables, and bread. They are also famous for their stews and roasts. And, when you go to Ireland, you can't forget the beer and whiskey. Even if you don't drink, the pub culture is fun and boisterous, as they are full of interesting people, stories, and great service.

In Irish culture, religion is very important and is often the center of festivals and other celebrations. Ireland is also very proud of a number of their sports, especially soccer, Gaelic football, rugby, hockey, and hurling.

The truth is, there are so many amazing pieces to Ireland's culture that it's hard to fit them all into one travel guide. Some cities such as Dublin need a travel guide of their own, as it has amazing culture all its own. If you're interested in learning about new and different cultures, Ireland is definitely a great place to check out. Not only are the sights amazing, but they are also integral to the island's culture and history.

St. Patrick's Day

Of course, one of the most well-known Irish holidays is St. Patrick's Day. This day often includes people celebrating by drinking green beer and wearing tall green hats. If you know anything about Ireland's culture, you know that this is one of the biggest Irish celebrations.

While the mascot for St. Patrick's Day is generally a leprechaun or a Shamrock, this day holds a special place in the heart of the Irish. In Ireland, it's a feast day where they celebrate Patrick, the man who brought Christianity to Ircland. When Patrick discussed the Holy Trinity, the Shamrock became part of this story because it was used as an example when explaining the Holy Trinity (the father, the son, and the Holy Spirit).

Irish immigrants would later bring St. Patrick's Day celebrations to North America with them, just like Halloween.

Irish Dancing

In the late 1900s, Irish dancing became popular outside of Ireland. The main reason for the rise in Irish dancing in many other countries, such as the United States, is due to Riverdance. However, Irish dancing is also popular due to how unique it is. One of the first ways to tell an Irish dance is by the lively, original costumes worn by the dancers. The Book of Kells is the inspiration for the dresses. Of course, you can't forget about the special tap dancing shoes which give each dance a special touch.

Irish Music

If you've never listened to Irish music, now is the time. Celtic music can be some of the most relaxing music in the world. Of course, you probably know about famous Irish bands, such as U2.

When you travel to Ireland, you will get a taste of a variety of different music. It's a popular topic, not just in pubs, where live bands play in almost every one of them, but it's also one of Ireland's favorite culture pieces.

While you might think of music as guitars, drums, and piano, Ireland takes its music one step further as they also play a dozen of other instruments. A lot of the music you hear from Ireland has a mix of home-grown instruments and the fiddle, along with the typical instruments played in a band. The Celtic Harp and Uilleann Pipes are also very popular choices.

Legends and Myths of Ireland

While you may read about myths and legends of Ireland online, when you visit, you will definitely need to hear the stories told from the Irish themselves. Without a question there's no one who can tell these stories better than the people who actually live there.

Of course, the most famous legend is that of the leprechaun. Whenever you think of a leprechaun, you might think of a pot of gold at the end of every rainbow. You might also think of a short creature in a green jacket and a tall green hat that is known to be untrustworthy.

In Ireland, you will see statues of leprechauns all over the country. Like all their other myths and legends, the Irish hold this close to their hearts and are very proud of it.

Sports/Recreation

Soccer

While soccer isn't the most popular sport in Ireland, it's Ireland's most well-known sport around the world and the sport people often enjoy seeing when they visit the island. Even though it's not Ireland's biggest sport, they are still proud of their teams. In Ireland, soccer is split into two leagues, one for the Republic of Ireland, and the other for Northern Ireland. On top of this, Irish soccer fans are believed to be some of the most welcoming in the world.

Horse Racing

In Ireland, Horse racing is considered more like a business as people use the sport to make bets and win money. Horse racing isn't considered to be highly recreational or even a sport used for passing the time. However, it's still one of Ireland's most popular sports, as it is enjoyed by people of all ages, with several horse races throughout the year.

Rugby

Rugby is probably the most popular sport in many parts of Ireland. And, while you should certainly watch as much live sports as you can, people often say that one of the games that you really have to go see is definitely Rugby. Rugby is similar to both soccer and football. In Rugby, there are two teams which play against each other. The players can either carry, kick, or throw the ball in order to score a goal between two posts.

Gaelic Games

The Gaelic Games are an amazing way to get involved in Irish culture. These are a collection of Ireland's popular games organized by the Gaelic Athletic Association (GAA). This association was created in the 19th century because the founders noticed that Irish sports were dying out. This was something they desperately wanted to change. Their endeavor paid off, as two of the Gaelic Games, Gaelic football and hurling, are some of the most popular sports in Ireland today.

The finals for Gaelic games, such as football and hurling are in September and attract well over 80,000 people. On top of this, the regular games, which are played in various Irish towns over the weekends have an attendance that averages about 40,000 people.

Chapter 3:
Why You Should Go To Ireland

There are so many reasons to visit Ireland that I can't possibly cover them all in this chapter of the book. Not only is Ireland home to dozens of castles (you will literally find castles everywhere when you visit Ireland) but the island is also home to some of the oldest pubs in the world! In addition there are the Cliffs of Moher, the 1,000 miles of the Wild Atlantic Way, great food, amazing scenery with some of the greenest grass and trees you will ever see in your life, and of course, the city of Dublin! In fact, when you start to plan your trip to Ireland, you will wonder how to even decide where to go because there are so many different and amazing locations to visit. But don't worry, this travel guide will help you learn which sites you should check out and how you can see several attractions through some of Ireland's special tours.

It is true that some people want to visit Ireland because of the beer, some want to visit it due to its heritage, while others want to visit it because they are interested in the culture and other aspects of Ireland. However, even though you might already have your own reasons to visit Ireland, below is a list of several other magical and amazing reasons to visit.

Ireland Has Amazing Castles

Who wouldn't like to see castles? Whether you're into majestic or gothic castles, in Ireland, you will find both. Best of all you won't have to look too hard to find a castle in Ireland due to the fact they are practically everywhere. Some are near the cities, and some are placed far away from any major civilizations out in the country. On top of this, you can even spend the night in some of these castles! Not only is this a way to see some Irish history, but it also allows you to imagine what it would be like to live in one of these castles as a king, queen, or knight. Not only can you get a glimpse of the romantic feel of castles, but you can also get a glimpse of their dungeons. Yes, these are the same dungeons that you read about in books and see pictures of online or in Hollywood movies. It's the next best thing to experiencing the island's past firsthand.

County Cork is home to Blarney Castle, one of the most famous castles in the world, with hundreds of thousands of visitors a year. But why is this castle so famous? Well, it is because of the legend of Blarney Castle, a tale that has been around for generations and that has often made its ways into the ears and minds of Ireland's visitors. The legend of Blarney Stone says that if you kiss the Blarney Stone, you will be rewarded with the gift of eternal eloquence. Because of this legend, visitors flock to Blarney Castle and do anything in their power to be able to kiss the castle's famous rock set.

And then, of course, there are the views. Castles in Ireland have some of the most breathtaking views you could possibly imagine. Visitors frequently go out of their way to ensure they can reach as high as possible to get the best view affordable of the castle grounds. Aside from great views and architecture, some castles even have dark and mysterious underground caves. Finally, you don't want to forget to check out the castle's fabulous gardens! Here you will find some of the most vibrant, luscious, and well manicured greenery that you have ever seen in your life.

Dublin, the crown jewel of Ireland

For many people, one of the best reasons to go to Ireland is to visit Dublin. It is one of the most talked about places in the world, and once you visit it, you'll never forget why! Dublin is the capital of Ireland and it's one of its greatest cities, which is pretty amazing considering the fact that Ireland is full of plenty of amazing cities! However, Dublin is slightly different. In fact, Dublin is actually a little different from many of the other cities that tourists and globetrotters find themselves in. While many cities travelers visit tend to get a bad reputation due to either its bad weather or because it doesn't offer much, this does not hold true for Dublin at all!

When people visit Dublin, they immediately talk about the town's personality. They discuss the many sights you can see, from museums to pubs. But this isn't all that Dublin has to offer, as it also provides such a great deal in terms of culture and entertainment. Dublin really offers something for everyone, because on top of all this, it also offers an impressive style of architecture that you won't find anywhere else.

But it doesn't stop here, as I haven't even talked about one of the best parts of Dublin yet! And trust me, when you go, this deal will be something that you won't want to pass up. It's called a Dublin Pass, and once you have it, you are able to visit about 30 of Dublin's biggest and best attractions for free! Yes, that's right - for free. But that's not all the Dublin Pass includes. You can also use it to gain discounts for a variety of businesses in the Dublin area, from theaters, restaurants, shops, transportation, and tours. And on top of all this (yes, there is one more thing), you get a free city guidebook! With all the things Dublin has to offer, you'll want to make sure to grab a copy.

Don't Forget About Irish Folklore

When you go to Ireland, you will learn about Irish folklore, and this is something you'll want to take in as much as you can, as it is just as intriguing and wonderful as the Irish scenery. Ireland is known for its many folklores, which include fairies, mermaids, leprechauns, and messages from butterflies. Yes, folks. Butterfly messengers. You see in Irish folklore, it's believed that butterflies deliver messages on behalf of fairies. Pretty crazy right? The colors of the butterfly have different meanings. For example, if you see a white butterfly, you will have stability in your life and generally receive good news. If the butterfly is yellow, you will find success. Of course, this is only one of Ireland's many folklore stories. They also have stories about leprechauns, Bram Stoker's influence for his famous *Dracula* novel (more on that later), and so much more! One of the best ways to learn about Irish folklore is to visit Ireland and hear the stories straight from your tour guides or when you visit the local pubs. The Irish folk love to discuss their folklore and legends late at night in a busy and cozy Irish pub! And with such rich material who could blame them!

Everyone Should Have An Irish Adventure

There simply isn't anything like an Irish adventure! It's an experience of culture, food, history, architecture, and tourist attractions. In fact, take a few moments to look through the pictures in this travel guide, or to Google and search for pictures of Ireland. Take in the scenery, buildings, culture, food, and everything else you find in the picture. Now, take a moment to imagine actually seeing this in person. You're in Ireland and you're standing right in front of the Blarney Castle or walking along the famous Grafton Street. In Ireland, you can easily get close to nature as you go mountain biking, sea kayaking, and rock climbing. When you're in Ireland, you get to take in the unique smells of the environment, whether it's the food as you're walking past a restaurant or just the scent of the island's flowers. You will also get to hear the sounds, from music to other live performances. Yes, you can listen to the sounds from your phone, but think about actually being there and experiencing these sounds firsthand as you take in all the smells, and tastes Ireland has to offer. Trust me, no matter how many pictures and videos you see, nothing is like actually going on your *own* Irish adventure!

There is No Scenery Like Irish Scenery

Enjoying Ireland's scenery is part of the adventure. Due to its astounding beauty, Irish scenery just can't be compared to anywhere else. You may have already witnessed its beauty in amazing postcards and pictures. However, seeing it in person will leave you breathless. It will get you relaxed and give you a sense of peace that you won't get anywhere else. You will get to see places dating as far back as the 12th and 13th Centuries, and if you put that into perspective – that is around 9 centuries ago! You won't find such amazing historic structures in many other places.

Two Words: Irish Food

In Ireland, food is always a tasty treat. Some of the best foods to try in Ireland include soda bread, Irish stew, boiled bacon and cabbage, seafood, coddle, and black and white pudding. No matter where you are in Ireland, the seafood is amazing; however, many tourists and residents claim that the closer you are to the ocean, the better the seafood is, which makes perfect sense. To find out for yourself, its highly recommended you try an assortment of restaurants located in different places. Irish stews are a tasty meal or can serve as a hearty appetizer made of different meats, potatoes, mutton, and onions. Lastly, the stews are topped with a delicious layer of vegetables and seasoning.

No Matter Where You Look, You'll Find History

One of the richest areas of Ireland is its history. When you visit Ireland, you have such an amazing choice of historical sites and interests that you probably won't even have enough time to visit them all! One of the most popular historical places is Newgrange, a prehistoric monument over 5,000 years old that served as a passage tomb. A few times a year, if you're inside the chambers, you can actually see what they look like. Doing so will allow you to see what the view was like hundreds of years ago. This has become such an attraction that a lottery is held just for access! Of course, this isn't the only historical place to visit. The Bru na Boinne in County Meath is also one of the most popular attractions. The Bru na Boinne is a very ancient location, and is known for being even older than Egypt's Pyramids of Giza and England's Stonehenge!

You Can Experience Pub Culture

Of course, when people think of Ireland, one of the main things that comes to their minds are Irish Pubs. All the major online travel sites, such as Lonely Planet, speak highly of Ireland's pub culture, and once you set foot into an Irish Pub, you will completely understand why. Irish pubs are almost always filled with music, great conversation, friendly patrons, delicious stouts and lagers, and great food. The popular Guinness Pie is a definite must.

There is a Guinness Storehouse

If you're interested in Ireland's pub culture, you can't forget about the Guinness Storehouse! Guinness is probably Ireland's most famous beer, and one of the many things to do in Ireland is to visit their plant! The storehouse, located at St. James Gate Brewery in Dublin, produces over 3 million pints a day, and is visited by over 1 million people a year! If you take a tour of the Guinness Storehouse, you'll get a behind the scenes look at what it takes to make some of Ireland's most famous beer. Not only will you be able to get a sample of Guinness right after it's produced, but you will also be able to see the brewing process and experience the steps it takes to get this product out to pubs in Ireland and all around the world. But don't think the Guinness storehouse hospitality stops there, as you will also get a chance to try some fabulous Irish food and some light refreshments.

Makes for Easy Travel All the Way Round

While we will discuss how to get to and around Ireland later on, one of the many reasons Ireland is such a fun place is because of how simple it is to travel there. You can get to Ireland by plane, ferry, a cruise, or you can even mix them up. When you are already in Ireland, you can use public transportation nearly everywhere, except in the countryside. Don't worry though, this doesn't mean that you'll miss out on any of Ireland's fantastic beautiful scenery or its country castles (you will later see that you can even stay in a castle). Also, you can get around Ireland by renting a car. However, you will see that there are situations where you need to be careful.

Of course, you can also get around Ireland by cruise, and you don't want to miss out on the many day tours that Ireland offers (more on this later). One of the great things about Ireland is that the officials of Ireland make sure there are various ways to get around the island for the travelers. This is often an important feature for tourists as sometimes one of the hardest factors about being a tourist is being able to travel from one attraction to the next. Fortunately, Ireland's visitor centers and officials have created multiple ways for tourists to see as many attractions as possible. For example, not only can you take a cruise to see parts of Ireland, but you can also take a bus or train around the city. The only area that you will struggle in if you don't have your own vehicle is in the country. However, officials in Ireland have continued to make transportation even more accessible so that tourist don't have to rent a car if they don't want to. For example, some tourist transportation businesses in Ireland have established a variety of tours that take tourists all around Ireland. We will discuss these tours later on in this travel guide. After you read it, you will surely be one of the many tourists to jump on a plane and head to Ireland

Ireland is Home to the Wild Atlantic Way

When you travel to Ireland, The Wild Atlantic Way is another must see. Ireland has a ton of iconic sights, and this is definitely one of them. The Wild Atlantic Way is 1,500 miles long, stretching from County Cork to County Donegal. Along the way, you will see other amazing sights, such as the Cliffs of Moher, beaches, towns, and amazing bays.

Giant's Causeway

Another sight that offers a once in a lifetime experience is the Giant's Causeway. This wonderful sight is filled with basalt columns which have inspired a great many people over the years, especially artists. Take a tour there to unlock the mystery that surrounds Giant's Causeway and to find out if any of the myths you might hear about or read about it online are true. You can either have a tour guide or choose instead to go it alone and rely solely on an audio system.

The Irish are Very Friendly

When you read reviews for Ireland, one of the things you will constantly see repeated is praise for Irish customer service and overall friendliness. While some of them might feel a little overwhelmed by all the tourists, they are still possibly some of the nicest people you will ever meet. They understand that Ireland is one of the most amazing places to visit and want tourists to enjoy their experience as much as possible.

If you've traveled before, you completely understand how wonderful it is to have helpful and friendly people as tour guides or to help you when you don't know what food to order. Sometimes, tourists can be a little shy when it comes to this, as they don't want to actually come across as a tourist. Thankfully, the majority of people in Ireland don't care that you're a tourist and will want to make sure you enjoy your experience so that you actually will want to come back to Ireland in the future.

Chapter 4:

Best Time To Go

Every traveler wants to know how the weather will be at their destination; in Ireland, the weather can be as much of an adventure as the overall Irish experience. What I mean by this is that Ireland is known for its unpredictable weather, which is why when you go to Ireland, you will hear many people talk about it. However, it's also known for its usually perfect temperatures, especially if you're from an area where you deal with low temperatures and low wind chills in the winter months, such as North Dakota and Minnesota. When you are used to minus 15 degrees with a wind chill of minus 20, making the temperature feel closer to minus 45 degrees, Ireland's average of 46 degrees seems absolutely lovely.

However, Ireland's weather should never hold you back from visiting any time of the year, as the unpredictable weather is all part of the Irish adventure. Even if you travel to Ireland during one of its rainy months, you'll find that it's still absolutely beautiful as the rain can help make the trip more soothing. Imagine sitting in a famous Irish pub, having one of the best meals you've ever had, with the slight tapping of rain on the roof, bringing a sense of calmness to the whole experience. Then, when you look, you will see that the rain helps make sure Ireland remains as beautiful as it is.

Having said that, people say that the best time to visit Ireland is during the spring months of April, May, and June. If you would rather travel in the fall, September and October are great months to visit too. However, this should never discourage you from visiting in the other months of the year, as no matter when you do, you'll be able to take in so much of Ireland that you'll always have a great adventure.

If you want to take in as much as Ireland's scenery as possible and not have to focus on some of island's heaviest tourist months, you will want to visit in the fall, winter, or spring. During these times, your adventure in Ireland can become a little more intimate because you feel closer to the attractions, weather, and overall Irish environment. One of the reasons you will feel closer to the attractions is because you will be able to spend more time there. Because there will be fewer people, you will be able to view and learn about them as much as possible. When you visit Ireland during the high season, you don't often get to view a lot of the attractions due to large crowds. You also learn less about the attraction because you don't have as much time to talk to the tour guide as they are busy with all the tourists. Another plus about traveling at times when Ireland's peak tourist season has ended is that you will find many deals, including cheaper hotel prices. No matter where you go in the world, if you travel during high season, hotels are going to raise their rates. However, if you travel during the low (off peak) season, hotels are more likely to have lower rates. Therefore, traveling to Ireland in the low season will allow you to save a significant amount of money.

No matter when you visit Ireland, you want to plan for all types of weather because Irish weather is unpredictable. Basically, you always want to make sure that you pack a light coat, sweater, pants, shorts, and a t-shirt. It's just all part of the great Irish experience!

Ireland Month By Month

To help you get a better sense of how great Ireland is throughout the whole year, despite the weather, let's take a look at what to do in Ireland, depending on the month that you visit. One of the great things about Ireland is that no matter what month you visit, there will always be some fun and exciting events going on!

January

January is a great time to visit because, while it's cool and rainy, it can also be very intimate. Also, it is known as a shoulder month, which means it's not a peak tourist month. On top of this, Christmas shopping and the tourist season is over. Because this you can spend more time viewing the sights in greater detail and getting a sense of Ireland's true winter culture.

Don't think that just because it's January, there are hardly any events or sights to see. As some places have winter hours and the days are shorter, this gives you a chance to enjoy the inviting Irish indoor culture. It gives you more of an opportunity to not just meet more people and have long conversations with them, but also to cozy up with a blanket in your hotel as you take in the Irish vibes.

While the dates change from year to year, Ireland is home to the Temple Bar Tradfest, celebrating Irish culture in a music festival. Ireland really knows how to make the colder days of the year "warmer" by celebrating their culture! This type of festival is sometimes one of the best ways to get a glimpse of it, but not only will you be able to meet many Irish residents, but also other tourists.

February

If you're interested in Irish Pubs, February is a great month to visit because you'll be able to spend a lot of cozy time in pubs while getting a taste of Irish culture, literally and figuratively. Even though the weather is around 40 degrees, this temperature is a dream for many. During this time, you will get some of the best hotel deals in Ireland, and you will still be able to see Gothic and historical castles, as well as many other places. Ireland is full of great museums, and with less of the tourist crowd, you'll be able to get up close and personal with Irish history.

On top of this, Ireland still has many events in February. For example, there's Shrove Tuesday, which is basically a Pancake Day. Yes, if you love pancakes, you should definitely check out Ireland in February! This also marks the start of Lent, which can often fall at the end of February or the beginning of March. Valentine's Day is another great day to be in Ireland as you can go see the Whitefriar Street Carmelite Church and the shrine of Saint Valentine, which is located in Dublin. The Whitefriar

Street Carmelite Church, which is also known as Church of Our Lady of Mount Carmel, is considered to be one of the most romantic places in Ireland, which is why visiting this location is even more amazing on one of the most romantic days of the year. Saint Valentine the Martyr's body is contained in the shrine. The Whitefriar Street Carmelite Church and the shrine of Saint Valentine is a popular location for couples because they believe that if they go to the shrine and pray to Saint Valentine, he will watch over them.

March

You probably know that one of the most famous Irish events, Saint Patrick's Day, is in March. Ireland's businesses, such as pubs and stores, also take part in the great day, which falls on March 17. During Saint Patrick's day, you will see a peak in visitors in the bigger cities of Ireland, such as Dublin, as everyone wants to take in the festivities. If you choose to visit in March, or throughout the year, you can also visit Christchurch Cathedral or Cliffs of Moher. Even though more tourists tend to come visit in March, it's still considered a shoulder season month because it's not one of the months that is most packed with tourists. Most tourists who come during March stay for St. Patrick's Day because they want to experience this Irish holiday. If you're looking to visit Ireland during one of the Shoulder Season months, March is a good choice because you will get a feel of Irish culture and history by attending Ireland's most spectacular holiday!

April

In April, tourists start flocking to Ireland again. As the days become longer, the temperatures start to rise to up to 50 to 60 degrees Fahrenheit. If you enjoy reading, Ireland is a great place to visit in April as you can attend the One City One Book festival, an event where residents and tourists all take part in reading one book. In April, other festivities include Easter and April Fools Day.

May

As the month of May comes around, Ireland gets a little warmer. Not only is the temperature heating up, so are the festivities and tourism. In Ireland, May 1st is a public holiday known as International Workers Day or Labor Day. Some workers' unions in Ireland will take this time to organize and host events focusing on the workforce in Ireland. Because it's a public holiday, businesses may be closed, but there will be celebrations and around this time, other tourist attractions will start to open up.

May 16th is another big day for Irish festivals as Ireland celebrates Saint Brendan of Clonfert, who claims to have discovered America. As an Irish saint, he's held in high regard and celebrated in some of the biggest festivals. This particular day is known as a feast day, so between the food, music, and other festivities planned, you will be able to get a nice taste of Irish culture.

June

Because this is the first summer month for many kids around the world, during this time, Dublin often starts to attract large tourist crowds. The weather is warm, and it's a joy to see Ireland buzzing with the sounds of tourists. Of course, hotels and other accommodations will use this as an excuse to hike up their prices, but this doesn't mean that you have to pay those. Just like other hotels, rates tend to change and if you book your trip early enough, you won't have to worry about this. Also, you won't have to worry about the hotel running out of space. Because there are so many tourists during this month, if you don't book early, you might have trouble finding a place to stay.

On June 16th of every year, an event known as Bloomsday takes place. This day is in honor of James Joyce and his novel *Ulysses*, which was published in 1922. The story takes place on June 16, 1904 in Dublin and focuses on characters such as Leopold Bloom. When people celebrate Bloomsday, they often dress up in the clothing of that time period. They further honor the novel and author by going to places written about in the book and eating the type of food that the characters ate at the time. The first Bloomsday took place in 1954 and it has only grown in popularity since.

July

If you like long days and warmer weather, with temperatures averaging around 60 degrees to 70 degrees Fahrenheit, you might want to visit Ireland in July. The sun normally doesn't set until around 11 pm, and like in other months, Ireland is filled with things to do and attractions to visit.

One of the main events in July is the Galway Arts Festival, which usually takes place during the second half of the month. You can buy tickets to see concerts, plays, and other events. Also, there is the battle of the Boyne, another event focused on Northern Ireland. This event is a celebration to honor a battle during the Glorious Revolution. Today, it's known as one of the biggest events in the history of Ireland. Even though the battle took place on July 1, 1690, it is celebrated on July 12th, a public holiday. Throughout the day, there are parades, food, games, and other fun things to do.

August

In Ireland, August is another month filled with adventure. While it does have its warm days, the temperature is nothing like the heat waves many other areas in the world face. It's warm, but if you're near the ocean, you get a nice ocean breeze to help make the day even better.

August has its fair share of festivals and celebrations. The Dublin Horse Show is often a crowd favorite in August, along with Rose of Tralee, which is a talent and beauty pageant to find the most Irish little girl of them all. This is a competition where little girls compete and show off their Irish culture. Whoever the judges feel is the most Irish of them all is the winner. The Puck Fair in County Kerry usually falls in the middle of August, and you won't want to miss out as this is an opportunity to experience an Irish fair, and even to see a goat crowned king! If you're in the area during this time, this is a must see as it's one of Ireland's oldest events. On August 15th, the whole island of Ireland holds a special Catholic Mass for the Feast Day of the Assumption of Mary.

September

In September, with school beginning again all around the world, the tourist season in Ireland starts to die down. This means that some touristic places such as the castles decrease their prices and accommodation can be easier to find, even in the last minute. This means that you could just drive around Ireland to check out sites and stay at any random hotel that's close to where you want to stop for the night.

In September, with fall starting to set in, the weather is still beautiful. In Dublin, on the first Sunday of September, The All Ireland Hurling Finals are held. Also, if you're in the area a couple of weeks after, you can check out the All Ireland Football Finals, which are held in the same location on the 3rd Sunday of the month. Ireland also likes to honor its farmers in September with the National Ploughing Championships, with 2019 being its 88th year running. It is always great fun to watch the plowing competition. You can also get a fun taste of Ireland's food and culture by checking out the farming equipment, the contest itself, and animals.

October

Of course, when people think of October, they think of Halloween, which originated in Ireland. However, in Ireland, it's often referred to as Samhain, and it doesn't begin until sundown (which is the reason people in America don't trick or treat until evening). Also, during the month of October, you can check out the Wexford Festival Opera, which will be in its 68th year in 2019. Also, The Moira Model Show, a crowd favorite, takes place at the end of the month.

So even when temperatures in Ireland start to cool down, with the average temperature ranging in the mid-50s, Ireland is still fairly busy with tourists. On top of this, you will start to find more great deals as Ireland's main tourist season has pretty much come to a close.

November

Even though some attractions and hotels in the country start to close as the winter season begins, it is also when Ireland starts to become a really cozy and quiet place. However, this doesn't mean that are attractions fully closed for the season. For example, sometimes, the visitor centers located at the attractions are closed, but you are still able to go in and check out the attraction itself. If you have any questions, you'll just have to find some locals to ask at your accommodation, or in a pub or restaurant. Of course, you can always do your own research on the attraction.

While the weather continues to get a little colder, yet still quite cozy, on November 11th, you can get a look at how the Irish celebrate Saint Martin's Day. This day exists to honor the man known as Martin le Miséricordieux or Martin of Tours. There are many famous stories about Saint Martin's kindness and generosity but the most famous one is how he cut his cloak in half so he could help keep a beggar warm during an unusually cold night in Ireland around the mid to late 300s A.D.

December

If you visit Ireland during the month of December, you're going to get a taste of the busy Christmas shopping season. As everybody is getting ready for Christmas, shoppers are spread all throughout Dublin, and it's really a magical time to see the city. While this is a great time to cozy up in Dublin to watch the sites and get a taste of Christmas, it is not the best time to shop for clothes, as many stores will take this time to hike up their prices.

Of course, December 25th and 26th are special days, with Christmas Day on the 25th and Boxing Day or Saint Stephen's Day the following day. Also, in December, another event that Ireland takes pride in is the Winter Solstice.

Shoulder Season

Shoulder Season, which is basically the off-season for tourists, is a special time in Ireland. Shoulder Season is during the months of April, May, June, October, and into the winter months. Basically, it includes any month that is not during peak summer months. While we've already discussed Shoulder Seasons in the previous months, let's now look at this in a little more detail.

During these months, the weather is still reasonably warm and cozy. The sights are still gorgeous, and as peak season has ended, the Irish are more likely to spend a large amount of time outside their homes. On top of this, you can still get the opportunity to see most of the tourist attractions, especially if you go in the months of April, May, and October. As a special bonus, during Shoulder Season, you will find some great deals on accommodations, transportation, and even the Dublin Day Pass.

When you spend some time by the fireplace in some of Ireland's restaurants and pubs, you will find that the staff is even more friendly than usual, because they have time to sit down and chat with tourists as the busiest season has ended. Just like you're interested in Irish culture, they're interested in your culture too, and they enjoy a good conversation.

One great thing about Ireland's Shoulder Season is that you will be able to see attractions without being around large crowds. All the outdoor attractions such as the cliffs will be wide-open to make your memory of the adventure, along with your photograph, picture perfect.

Chapter 5:
Weather Throughout The Year

Whenever someone travels, one of their first thoughts is typically something like "I wonder what the weather will be like?" If you are wondering this about Ireland, look no further, because this chapter will give you all the information you need.

In Ireland, you can live through all four seasons in one day. While I am sure some of you reading this from the northern states of America, such as Minnesota, North Dakota, and Wisconsin think that this isn't possible because not even your state goes through those type of weather changes, and your state is known for crazy and quick weather changes. Well, it actually is possible; within a 24 hour period, Ireland can go through all four seasons (spring, summer, fall, and winter). But this doesn't mean you should second guess your trip to Ireland. It just means that you just need to get ready for a fun and exciting trip to Ireland with unpredictable weather!

In Ireland, the weather is never too hot or too cold. So, even though you have to pack for all types of weather, you won't have to deal with any extremes. The reason why there are never really any extreme weather conditions is because of the Atlantic Ocean, which influences Ireland's weather.

The Perfect Time To Visit

There is no perfect time to visit Ireland because it all depends on your personal preference. This is completely normal as everyone has their favorite time to travel to a particular country. The point I want to make here is that you don't want to put off traveling because you feel the weather will be too cold. You want to pick a time to travel to Ireland that is 100% suited for you! This might mean going in January or February when Ireland's weather is cold because you want to spend as much time as you can in tourist attractions. January and February, along with the other Shoulder Season months, are great times to go because there are fewer tourists. Therefore, you're able to spend more time learning about a tourist destination and seeing the sights without having to go through large crowds. Or, perhaps you might want to go when the weather is warmer and during peak tourist months, like in summer. As I mentioned before, Ireland is full of things to do, from visiting museums to checking out festivals. It doesn't matter if it's in the middle of winter or the middle of summer, because Ireland will always find a reason to celebrate and give tourists a taste of Irish culture.

The Weather of the Seasons

Spring and summer months, which range from February to July, include long days and warm sun. In Spring, the temperature ranges from around 45 degrees to 54 degrees

Fahrenheit, while in Summer, it ranges from 64 degrees to 68 degrees Fahrenheit. If you prefer longer days, your best time to visit will be towards the end of Summer and beginning of Fall, in the months of July and August, as the sun doesn't set until around 11 PM!

Many tourists and Irish residents state that April is a very pleasant month. If you're traveling to Ireland in the Spring, you will probably want to make sure to carry a light jacket with you, like a springtime waterproof jacket or windbreaker. In the summer months, it wouldn't hurt to carry a light waterproof coat with you either! You may get a taste of Irish rain. Just another fun adventure in Ireland!

During the fall and winter months, which range from August until January, the temperature ranges from 54 degrees to 64 degrees Fahrenheit in the Fall, while in the Summer, it averages 46 degrees. And if you're not a fan of snow, you're going to love visiting Ireland during the winter, because it hardly snows there!

The fall months are mostly warm, but around October to November, the temperature slowly starts to decrease, which is when winter sets in. Just like when traveling in the spring or summer, you'll want to bring a light coat or sweater with you. If you travel to Ireland in the winter months, remember to carry a heavier coat. And make sure to stop in some cozy pubs (the ones with fireplaces are great!).

The Key is the Wardrobe

No matter what month you visit Ireland, you're going to have an adventure with the weather. It doesn't matter if you travel to Orlando, Florida, or France, you will probably see rain at some point during your vacation. No matter how hard we try, we always want to be prepared for unpredictable weather! However, when it comes to Ireland, rain just adds more beauty as you need rain in order for nature to grow. So, when it rains, instead of staying in a hotel room, go out and smell it. Then, find some indoor activities or visit a pub. The rain will probably quickly cease, as it doesn't usually rain for a long time at once in Ireland.

One of the most important things on your trip is to pack accordingly. You want to pack for Ireland's fun and unpredictable weather, so you will want to bring a sweater, even in the summer. It won't get too cold, but it can get a bit chilly. Also, you want to make sure you have some type of waterproof light coat or an umbrella for when it rains. And don't leave the sunscreen in the hotel! Even if you feel like it's cool and a little cloudy, the sun can still peak through those clouds and give you a sunburn. Also, when the sun is shining in Ireland, it gets hot, just like anywhere else, so you want to make sure you protect yourself. Make sure to pack comfortable shoes (you will do a lot of walking!), sunglasses, and any other type of clothing for outdoor activities. Basically, you'll want to dress in layers, as you can always take off some layers if you start to get a bit warm.

Tackle Ireland's Weather With These Tips

To prepare yourself for Ireland's unpredictable weather, it's a good idea to check the forecast. Nowadays, you can do so easily with an app on your phone. Who knows, you might find differences in the way Ireland talks about the weather over your home area. For example, Irish people know that their weather is unpredictable, so their weather forecasters might make jokes about the unpredictable weather, especially during the peak tourists months. The Irish like to have a good time and the Irish also want to make sure their tourists are having a good time. However, when you're in your own city, your weather forecasters might not be able to joke about the weather because it's not as unpredictable. Getting a glimpse of the way Ireland's media acts and comparing this to the way your local news media acts is another part of the Irish experience!

Another great tip to deal with the weather is to be prepared and take it as it comes. This means that you shouldn't complain about it. Even if you don't like rain, consider it another adventure in your vacation.

A third tip (and a way to meet someone who lives in Ireland) is to find out who farms and ask them the weather. Farmers always have their own ways to predict the weather, and they tend to be correct more times than not. For example, farmers tend to watch their animals to forecast the weather. If they see their animals crowding together in a group, they assume that rain or snow is coming. Farmers have these special ways to predict the weather, so if you meet one in a festival, museum, pub, or anywhere else, go ahead and ask them to forecast the weather. You can even have some good ol' Irish fun with this and see if the farmer's predictions turn out to be right. In Ireland, adventures are around every corner!

Chapter 6:

Estimated Costs of Your Trip

Before I start discussing the estimated cost of your trip, I want to tell you not to let the cost keep you away from the adventure. Of course, the cost of your trip will depend on how long you stay, how you plan to travel, where you stay, etc. Therefore, you want to remember that this chapter focuses on an estimate for a trip to Ireland. You will still need to create your own budget in order to get the proper cost. However, the estimated total given below can help you focus on what type of budget you will need to look at when planning your own trip to Ireland. The most important piece of information is not to let the price scare you away because Ireland is worth it!

Estimated Cost for One Person

For this first estimate, you're traveling by yourself from the United States to Ireland. You've decided to stay a week and found hotels and travel cost that was in the middle range of prices. This means the prices were average; not the highest, but not the lowest either.

Air travel (round trip)	$1,000
New Luggage	$120
A rental vehicle in Ireland	$800
Gas and Insurance for your rental	$200
Hotel for 6 nights	$550
Food and drinks	$300
Attraction admission	$200.00
Tourist buses and transportation	$300
Souvenirs and any extras	$400
Total	$3,870

As I said before, this is just an estimate. The trip could be cheaper or more costly, depending on where you stay and what type of car rental deal you find.

Estimated Cost for A Couple or Family

To get the estimate for a couple of people, you can simply double the estimate for one person. However, this is not entirely true, as you can sometimes get better deals if there is more than one person on your trip. Also, if you will have children with you, make sure to ask if there are any special prices for kids.

Travel Costs Explained

Accommodations

When it comes to accommodation, if you book early, you could find a good deal. Of course, another way to save money is to compare prices when looking at different cities you can stay in. While you might want to stay in an area like Dublin because there are so many sights to see, you will probably find better deals in other cities. If you want to see as much of Ireland as possible, you may want to consider staying in different accommodations while you move around.

Hotels are not your only option for accommodation. Here are a few other options:

- An Airbnb is often a cheap way to find accommodation in Ireland. While many people feel that Airbnb's are not safe, you can always make sure that it is in a safe area. That is one of the biggest tips that cannot be stressed enough; always make sure a location is safe. Research it thoroughly and find out if there is any crime reported in that specific area. Also, you can read reviews left from other users. Most Airbnb's, especially ones where they expect tourists, are extremely clean and safe. On top of this, the prices are the cheapest you may find.

- You might want to look at staying at an Irish B&B, even just for a night to get an idea of the culture. Ireland is known for its friendly service, and this is true for any Irish B&B. These accommodations tend to be very cozy and include delicious breakfasts, which always helps when you're traveling.

- Hostels are another option, although they are usually only for solo travelers. However, if your budget is very tight or you or just want to get in on this experience in Ireland for one night, the hostel may accommodate a couple of people. You can ask for a private room or go the cheapest route and get a bed in a dorm. Hostels can be a great experience, as you can meet many people there. This can always be part of your travel experience because you can learn about different people and their cultures. Who knows, they may even give you some travel tips.

- Staying in a Luxury Hotel is another option. If you can afford to stay at a luxury hotel for at least one night, I highly suggest sleeping in an Irish castle hotel! There are several amazing castle hotels to choose from. You could stay in Kinnitty Castle Hotel, Ballyseede Castle Hotel, Waterford Castle Hotel, Ballynahinch Castle, and many more! You will need to have rented a car though, because some of these castles are further out into the beautiful and stunning Irish countryside.

- Mid-Range Hotels are probably the main hotel's people use. They have a variety of rooms, prices, and deals. These hotels are typically very clean and have a variety of benefits included in the price of the room.

Airfare

You can always get a good deal on airfare. People generally plan their vacations far in advance, and the earlier you book, the cheaper your rate will be. On top of this, prices change with the seasons. For example, to save money, you don't want to fly on some of the busiest travel days of the year, such as Thanksgiving and Christmas, as flights will be more expensive. Also, you don't want to fly on St. Patrick's day. Remember that there will be busy days in the Summer months, starting around June until the end of August.

Another way to look for cheap airfare is just to check out places. You want to compare prices and see the cheapest flights you can get. These prices will change due to many factors, such as where you're flying out from and what country you live in. For example, people who live in Canada tend to have to pay more for their flights to Ireland than people who live in the United States.

The best times to head to Ireland are during Ireland's busy tourist off-season, especially in the Winter. As we have already discussed, it is always a great time to visit Ireland, even in January and February. However, tourists' favorite month is usually around Spring, in the months of April and May or in the Fall, in September and October. There are a couple of reasons for this. First, you won't have to deal with a lot of crowds. This will help you find time to really enjoy the sights and scenery. Also, everything is still open as the tourist season is winding up or down.

Transportation

Ireland is full of public transportation, which is a great way to see many of island's sights. However, if you don't want to follow the public transportation route or schedule or just want to see places of Ireland not on the route, you should look at renting a car.

Before renting a car, you want to make sure you understand the way people drive in Ireland. In the United States, we drive on the right side of the road, but in Ireland, it's on the left. Also, Ireland isn't big on automatic vehicles; you can rent one, but they are a bit more expensive than the standard vehicle. In addition, car rental companies don't keep a lot of automatic vehicles on hand, so you want to make sure there will be one available when you arrive. Also, you want to watch out for the sheep. Ireland is known for its sheep, and on many country roads, you might run into sheep just hanging around the road. Finally, if you're not very comfortable driving on country roads in the United States, you will probably be even less so in Ireland as they tend to be more winding and narrow. If you're thinking about driving in Ireland, you want to make sure you know the rules of the road along with other factors.

If you decide to stick with public transportation, you'll be able to visit any city in Ireland as they all have their own bus system. Of course, you can also travel using the train system. While both systems of public transportation work, you'll want to note a few differences between buses and trains. For example, buses are often cheaper. Also, you often tend to get to your destination a little quicker with the city bus than with the train. However, you can purchase your tickets ahead of time, which might be cheaper in some situations. On the other hand, if it's a spur of the moment trip, you can also purchase tickets right before you board.

Food

Food can be a bit expensive, with all three meals costing a little over $50 a day, but this does not include any snacks or drinks, and prices will always vary depending on where you are. However, when you try some of the food that Ireland is known for, such as their stew, you're going to understand why the prices aren't cheap. Adding any drinks to your meal is going to make the price go up considerably, and you can easily spend $20 a day on drinks in Ireland, especially if you chose to eat meals in pubs. To be on the safe side, you may want to add a little extra money to your food budget.

Attractions

While we will focus on attractions later in this travel guide, let's first talk about the pricing for those. If you want to see as much as possible, especially in Dublin, you can purchase a Dublin Pass, which allows you to save money and see about 30 sites in Dublin. To get one, head to www.dublinpass.com where you will find a page where they tell you exactly how to do so.[1] The first step is to go through their process, where you get to create your own Dublin Pass for your special trip. From there, you can decide to have the pass mailed to you or pick it up in Dublin when you arrive. Finally, when you are on vacation, you want to make sure to show your Dublin Pass

---

[1] "How Does The Dublin Pass Work?". Dublinpass.Com, https://www.dublinpass.com/what-you-get/how-it-works.html.

at different sites that you visit, as you'll be allowed in for free!

When you pay for your Dublin Pass, you pay for all of it at once and also save a lot of money on admission fees. You can choose from four different passes. While these are sometimes on sale, the average price for a day pass is $62 for an adult and $33 for a child. You can also get a two-day pass, which brings you up to around $80 for an adult and $40 for a child. Three-day Dublin Passes go up to $90 for adults and $50 for children. Finally, you can also get a five-day pass, which costs around $100 for adults and $60 for children.

What type of sales will a Dublin Pass get you? Of course, this depends on what places you want to visit. Some of the most popular attractions you can use the pass for are the Dublin Castle, which you save $8.00 for, the Dublin Zoo with savings of $18, St. Patrick's Cathedral with savings of $8.00, and Guinness Storehouse with savings of $25.00! You can also decide to visit these other popular attractions: (1) EPIC The Irish Emigration Museum with savings of $15.00. (2) Glasnevin Museum with savings of $7.00. (3) Hop on Hop off Bus Tour with a savings of $22.00. (4) Jameson Distillery, Bow. St with a savings of $22.00. (5) Christ Church Cathedral with a savings of $7.00. (6) Teelings Distillery with a savings of $17.00.

Extras

No matter how hard you try, you're always going to buy a few extras on your vacation. First, you're going to want to buy home souvenirs, and not just for yourself. You might have children, grandparents, grandchildren, best friends, or parents to buy things for. The only way you can really focus on your extras is to just budget some of your money for it. Of course, it's always hard to tell how much you're going to need. Sometimes, you can get a sense of this through what you've spent on other trips, and other times you can't. It also depends on what type of extras you find. If you really want to go all out, you'll want to put aside a few hundred dollars for this. However, if you're more into memories rather than material things, you should be OK with a couple of hundred dollars.

Chapter 7:

What To Pack

When you're thinking about what to pack for any vacation, there are many factors to consider, and for Ireland, whose weather can be unpredictable, this makes clothing choices a little harder. But think of it this way, no matter where you go, you want to be prepared for all types of weather as even in the summer months, temperatures can fall to 50 or even 40 degrees, while they're usually sitting at around 80 degrees. If you didn't pack a sweater, this can make for a very cold day!

The Necessities

Of course, the first thing you think of are the things you will really need. At first, this might seem a bit overwhelming. This is why we have broken down what to pack into different categories because let's face it, you're going to need to pack more than you realize, so to help you in your packing process, why not work on one list at a time.

Your necessities include your wallet or purse, which is a good place to store extra copies of your passport. Things happen for many reasons, so it's never a bad idea to have a passport copy just in case. You will also want to make sure this copy is handy and not in the same place as your passport.

Other items in the necessities list include:

- Important documents, such as your passport, visa, and any travel insurance. **Tip:** it's not a bad idea to make copies of these as well and keep them with the copy of your passport.

- Any medication you take on a daily basis. This not only includes the prescription medication you need but also any other over the counter medication, such as allergy medication or cough drops. On top of this, if you're planning on staying in Ireland for a long time, you will want to make sure you have enough medication with you. If you need a refill but your pharmacy won't fill it as it's too soon since your last refill, take the time to explain to your pharmacist who may be able to help you due to your travel arrangements. On top of this, you will want to carry extra copies of your actual prescriptions for your medication, just in case. Your pharmacist may be able to help you with this.

- You also want to look at what technology you're going to be packing as you will want to make sure you have all the compatible chargers and necessary attachments. Of course, we will take a second to look at this on our technology list, but it never hurts to stay a step ahead in your packing!

Personal Items

When it comes to personal items, you might feel overwhelmed, but there is nothing to worry about. You will want to keep these items close, and remember not to pack any sentimental items you would regret losing.

Ireland can be a bit of a long flight, depending on where you're flying out from. Because of this, it wouldn't hurt to have personal items you might need within a couple of days with you on your carry on bag. For your personal items that don't fit in your carry bag, you will want to make sure they are easily accessible from within your luggage. Another tip is to not pack these items in the same luggage your clothes are in, as sometimes things get lost. Of course, you want to follow airport guidelines too.

The following table is a checklist for personal items you should think about taking with you on your flight to Ireland. Of course, if you think of more items, you can pack them as well.

Liquid Bags	Small First Aid Kit	Sunscreen	Headphones
Change of clothes	Mints	Gum	Sunglasses
Fuzzy socks	Flip Flops	Lip balm	Unscented lotion
Makeup	Baby wipes	Antibacterial wipes	Travel Blanket
Scarf	Tissues	Toiletries	Contact Lenses and solution
Glasses and cleaner	Feminine hygiene products	Small flashlight	Travel towel
Deodorant	Toothbrush	Toothpaste	Shampoo (travel size)
Conditioner (travel size)	Soap	Grooming kit (if allowed on the plane)	

Packing for Adventurous Weather

As you've previously read, Ireland's weather is unpredictable, which means you want to plan for any type of weather. This means that even if you're traveling in Ireland's peak tourist season in the summer, you will want to bring a light windbreaker, a waterproof jacket, or a sweatshirt. Think of the age-old rule to traveling, which is "there's no such thing as bad weather, only bad clothing."[2] Another rule of thumb is to pack for three seasons. For example, if you're going in July, you won't need to pack any winter clothes, but you will want to pack a fall and spring type jacket along with sandals and solid shoes.

2

Ebert, S. What to Pack for Ireland - Tortuga Backpacks Blog. Retrieved from https://blog.tortugabackpacks.com/ireland-packing-list/.

The following table is a checklist for adventurous weather items you should think about taking with you on your flight to Ireland.

Raincoat/jacket	Comfortable closed-toe shoes	Sandals
Extra pair of shoes	Hat	Scarf
Sweater/Hoodie	Swim Suit	Umbrella
Gloves		

Packing Your Technology

In this day and age, we seem to not be able to go anywhere without our technology. Before you pack your technology for your trip, you want to talk to your cell phone company to see if you need to make any temporary changes to your plan. Also, it wouldn't hurt to have an extra charger in your carry on bag, just in case.

The following table is a checklist for technology items you should think about taking with you on your flight to Ireland. Of course, if you have more technology items than this, you can pack more things.

Power adapter	Necessary converters	Tablet and charger
Computer and charger	Portable charger	Camera and charger
Memory cards (for the camera)	External Hard drive	Wifi Hotspot

Clothing

While this was partly touched on in the adventurous weather list, you need still to pack more clothes. The adventurous weather list is just to help you pack clothes that suit the unpredictable Irish weather, but you're still going to need regular clothes to go along with this. Because Ireland tends to be pretty casual no matter where you go, you won't need to worry about fancy clothing, unless you know of a situation where you will need it. For example, you might be interested in going to a fancy night.

The following table is a checklist for clothing items you should think about taking with you on your flight to Ireland.

Of course, you can pack more if you can think of additional clothing items to bring with you. Some of these items will depend on how many days you're staying and if you plan to do laundry while during your vacation. For example, if you're staying six days and don't want to worry about laundry, it wouldn't hurt to bring seven pairs of socks; one for every day in Ireland, and an extra pair just in case.

Socks	Pants/jeans	Shorts
Underwear	T-shirt	Long sleeve shirts

Anything Extra?

Of course, whenever you pack, you will always want to get a few extra things. This is completely normal and fine, but just remember to follow the flight guidelines and not to take sentimental items with you.

The following table is a checklist of extra items you might want to bring with you to Ireland. Of course, this is just a checklist, and you can always bring a few more things.

Bug spray	Jewelry (remember nothing valuable or sentimental)	Workout gear	Journal
Pens/pencils	Noise cancelling headphones	Small binoculars	Reusable water bottle
Reusable shopping bags	Duct tape (If you're planning on camping)	Waterproof phone case	Packing cubes
Handy toiletry bag	Jet lag relief tablets		

What You Should Not Bring

Of course, just like on any trip, there are items that you shouldn't bring with you. Aside from items that you can't bring on the airplane, here are a few more items you won't need to pack. If you have a treasured item and feel the need to see it every day, just take a picture of it rather than bring it with you. You don't want to bring any valuable items as these can get lost on the trip.

Items of Sentimental Value

If something is sentimental to you, don't pack it. To help you follow this rule when deciding what to pack, don't pick things that you would regret losing. Don't pack items that you would never be able to replace and that hold strong emotional value. If you feel you would never be able to forgive yourself for losing a particular item, don't pack it.

Camouflage Clothing

This is mostly just a way to make sure you honor the members of the military the correct way. While wearing camouflage is ok, you don't want to be mistaken for a member of the military, and if your camouflage clothing looks like Irish DPM, it's illegal to wear it if you're not a member of the military on duty. Also, you will want to avoid camouflage clothing because people will be able to tell that you're a tourist and won't appreciate it, as their view is that only active military men should be wearing this.

Heavy Items

The reality is, you're going to be moving your luggage around, so you don't want it to be too heavy to carry. So, you want to make sure you don't overpack.

Expensive Items

Expensive items go along with the sentimental items, as they are something that you don't want to take because of their value. If you're bringing a really expensive camera, you'll want to make sure that you have your hand on it at all times or keep it in a place that will be hard for anyone to try to steal it.

I don't mean to say that violent crime is a big problem in Ireland, but this type of crime is possible anywhere, even in your own city. No matter where you travel, you want to take extra care of your items to make sure nothing is taken from you.

Fanny Packs

While some people might see this as more of a fashion no-no, it also makes it easy for pickpocketers. These thieves are often pros at their job, so you won't even notice or feel that they have taken anything. They could be talking right in front of you while coming up with a plan to get a hold of your fanny pack.

Chapter 8:

Methods of Travel

How to get to Ireland will be one of the most important points when organizing your trip. While we've already discussed the methods of travel once you get to Ireland, such as renting a car and the public transportation system, this travel guide hasn't touched on how to get to Ireland.

While you might think the only way you can go to Ireland is directly by flight, this is not entirely true. While the most popular method is air travel, you can go in different ways depending on where you live, like with a cruise or ferry.

Air Travel

Of course, the most popular way to travel to Ireland is by plane, as this is the quickest and most affordable way to get to Ireland. In Ireland, there are around ten airports scattered around the island. While there might be some travel time to get from the airport to your accommodation, most airports are within the main cities. And if you, plan your vacation well, you won't have to worry too much about going from the airport to your accommodation. Having said that, it is worth noting that most of the airports run along the coastline of Ireland, with no major airports in the center. So, while making plans to travel around Ireland, you will want to keep this in mind.

One of the busiest airports you can fly into is Dublin airport, which isn't too far north from the center of Dublin. If you want to travel around Ireland but know one of your big stops is going to be Dublin, it's a good idea to fly to or from Dublin. Other airports to look into include Belfast City Airport, Cork Airport, Kerry Airport, Ireland West Airport, Donegal Airport, Shannon Airport, Derry Airport, Belfast International Airport, and Waterford Airport. If you visit the Irish tourism website, you can find more information about each of these airports, including their location.[3]

Ferry

Another way to reach Ireland is by Ferry. In order to use the Ferry, you will need to travel to France, Wales, Spain, or England and use one of their ports.

Holyhead to Dublin Ferry

One of the most popular ferries is the Holyhead to Dublin Ferry. This route is so popular that its operation depends on two different ferry companies, with a total of 63 trips

---

[3]

"Airports In Ireland - Irishtourist.Com". Irishtourist.Com, http://www.irishtourist.com/travel-info/airports-in-ireland/.

per week. One of the Ferry services, the Irish Ferries service, runs for two hours a trip about five times a day. The other Ferry service, the Stena Line service, takes a little over 3 hours and runs about four times a day.

Liverpool to Dublin Ferry

You can also take the Liverpool to Dublin Ferry, which takes about 8 hours, with a dozen of trips a week. P&O Irish Sea is the Ferry service that operates this route and they sometimes make more trips during the week than other times. For example, they might run more than 12 trips a week in the summer, but fewer in low seasons.

Liverpool Birkenhead to Belfast Ferry

The Stena Line service also handles the Liverpool Birkenhead to Belfast Ferry. This service runs around 13 times a week and lasts around eight hours. Like the Liverpool to Dublin Ferry, it might run more trips some weeks than others. As of now, no other Ferry service runs this route, so you have to take the Stena Line Ferry service. But, like all of the Ferry services, is it top of the line, and the sights that you will see on your trip will be amazing!

Roscoff to Cork Ferry

Brittany Ferries is another service that brings people to Ireland. One of the routes this Ferry service runs is the Roscoff to Cork Ferry service. On average, this route runs around three times a week, and it takes about 14 hours to make the trip from France to Ireland. This Ferry service might not always run as it is only seasonal, so if this is something you are interested in, you will want to make sure that this line is running before you travel to Ireland.

Cairnryan to Larne Ferry

If you want to travel from Scotland to Ireland, one of the Ferry routes you can check out is the Cairnryan to Larne Ferry. Run by P&O Irish Sea Ferry service, it makes nearly 50 trips a week, depending on the time of the year. Each trip lasts around 2 hours.

Santander to Cork Ferry

This Ferry goes from Spain to Ireland and takes a little over 26 hours for a trip. So, if you really want to travel and take a long Ferry journey, this is one of the best choices. This route is run by Brittany Ferries, and it only runs a couple of times a week. Also, you will want to make sure that it's running during the off-season.

Take a Cruise

If you've always wanted to take a cruise, this could be your best chance. The Adventure-life website has a list of the top ten cruises in Ireland for the 2019-2020 season.[4] Not only does this website list the top ten cruises, but if you have any questions, you can also contact an expert. In addition, the website also has a list of deals you can look into.

European Classic Cruise to Ireland

The European Classic Cruise is one of the most popular ones on the list. It is a seven-day cruise which takes you to places such as Glasson to Athlone one day, Shannonbridge to Terryglass another day, and Mountshannon to Killaloe near the end of the week. On this cruise tour, you get to visit the Birr Castle Gardens and Science Center tour. You also get to see the sights of Kilbeggan Distillery and Leap Castle, which is believed to be one of Ireland's most haunted places.

Amsterdam to Dublin

Amsterdam to Dublin is an eleven-day cruise where you get to see the sights of St Peter Port, Guernsey, Cliffs of Moher, Killybegs, and Portrush. On top of this, you also get to tour the Kylemore Abbey, Tresco Abbey Gardens, and see the castles of Picton and Pembroke. Altogether, this cruise costs about $8,500.

---

[4] "10 Best Small Luxury Cruises To Ireland For 2019-2020 By Adventure Life". Adventure-Life.Com, https://www.adventure-life.com/ireland.

Ireland, Scotland, and Cornwall

Ireland, Scotland, and Cornwall is a thirteen-day cruise that costs around $7,000. On this cruise, you get to see several different sights, such as Killybegs, Galway, Ireland, Belfast, and Dartmouth. On top of this, during this 13-day journey, you're sure to learn all about Irish culture.

Chapter 9:

Currency in Ireland

When traveling to a different country, travelers often have questions about the currency For instance, you might ask yourself what type of currency Ireland uses and if you can use American dollars there. Well, we will address all these questions in this chapter. Also, we will talk about your ability to use your debit or credit cards while traveling in Ireland. As a special bonus, at the end of this chapter, I will discuss currency conversion apps. So, make sure to check out your special bonus!

Does all of Ireland use the same currency

No, not all of Ireland uses the same currency. There are two different currencies in Ireland, so when you travel there, you're going to want to make sure you're prepared for this. Of course, there will be people there to help you, so don't worry too much. Because Ireland is a touristic place, there are many tourist visitor centers that can help get you set up with these different currencies. Also, if you prefer, you can speak to your travel agent as they will know the steps you need to take.

Although the two countries in Ireland get along, they have a different currency. In Northern Ireland, they use what is known as the Sterling Pound, while in the Republic of Ireland, they use the Euro. When the Euro is spoken about as money, it's referred to as notes, similar to American dollars. The notes of the Euro are "€5, €10, €20, €50, €100, €200 and €500".[5] On top of this, the Euro system also has coins, just like the American system. Their "coins are 1c, 2c, 5c, 10c, 20c, 50c, €1 and €2."[6] With the Euro, another point to note is that most retail outlets will not accept big notes, meaning €100, €200 and €500 are not accepted at stores. Therefore, when you trade your country's money for Euros, it's best to make sure you have smaller notes.

The Sterling Pound has £5, £10, £20, £50 and £100 notes."[7] Just like the Euro, these are similar to American dollars. On top of this, the Sterling Pound system also has coins, which are in the following amounts "1p, 2p, 5p, 10p, 20p, 50p, £1 and £2."[8]

---

[5] Money in Ireland. Retrieved from https://www.ireland.com/en-us/about-ireland/must-know-information/money-in-ireland/.

[6] ibid.

[7] Money in Ireland. Retrieved from https://www.ireland.com/en-us/about-ireland/must-know-information/money-in-ireland/.

[8] ibid.

Can I use American Dollars In Ireland

The simple answer is no. When you go to Ireland, you have to either use the Sterling Pound or the Euro, depending on which part of Ireland you're in. If you're in the Republic of Ireland, you need to use the Euro, while in Northern Ireland, you need to use the Sterling Pound. Furthermore, these are generally not interchangeable. For example, you can't use the Euro in Northern Ireland, or the Sterling Pound in the Republic of Ireland. If you're traveling to both locations, you'll want to make sure you have each currency in hand. You can also do an exchange when you get into the other part of Ireland.

Can I use debit and credit cards in Ireland

Yes, you can use most credit cards in Ireland, such as Mastercard and Visa. American Express can be used in some places, but not everywhere. You can also use your debit card, as long as it is a Mastercard or Visa. You should be able to use it both in-store and to withdraw money from an ATM. Unlike in the United States where it's more common to use plastic, in Ireland, cash is king. You should also be aware that when it comes to debit and credit cards, Ireland has the pin and chip system. While a few retail stores may swipe your card, this is rarely done in both the Republic of Ireland and Northern Ireland.

Of course, it's always a smart idea to notify your credit card company and bank when you're about to travel so that you can tell them that you will be using your card in another country in order for them not to block it. This is a typical security measure, and they can quickly turn your card back on, but it saves the hassle of you trying to notify your bank or credit card company that you're in Ireland when your card stops working.

BONUS: List of Great Currency Apps

My Currency Converter

If you own an iPhone, this is one of the best apps to download to help you manage your money from anywhere, at any time. For many people, it's well liked because it's very simple to use, has graphs which are easy to understand, and is able to support around 150 currencies from all around the world. This is fabulous for anyone who loves to travel! On top of all these great benefits, the app will automatically update you when there is a change in currency rates. Also, My Currency Converter gives you some of the most accurate currency exchange rates because it uses 3 decimal places and converts the numbers as you type. It's always nice when there is one fewer button you need to worry about pushing.

Travel Calculator

The Travel calculator app is ranked in third place on the list of currency calculators. It's known as another very easy to use conversion calculator. However, unlike many other conversion calculators, the Travel Calculator also has a tip calculator installed. This means that no matter where you are, you can see how much you should tip your hostess. Many people who have used this calculator believe it's one of the easiest to use, and it has a nice, user-friendly layout.

All Currency Converter

While the All Currency Converter is rated fifth on the list of Currency Converter apps, some people feel that the layout is a little hard to understand. However, once you get the hang of what's going on, the app becomes very easy to use. This currency app is made for Android phones. Like many other currency converters, this app has over 160 currencies.

XE Currency

The XE Currency app is great because you can use it on both an Android and an iPhone. On top of this, the XE Currency converter gets updated automatically with new exchange rates and will work offline, unlike many other currency converters. However, you need to remember to download the currency rates before you head out on your trip.

Currency Convert

Many exchange rate apps request that you download any current currency exchange rates you need before heading out to your destination. But this isn't the case for the Currency Convert, which has exchange rates for more than 160 currencies. This iPhone app is widely known as one of the easiest currency exchange apps available.

Currency Pro

Currency Pro is a newer Iphone app that was released in 2018. This app is rated number ten on the list of Currency Converters. Because it is new, there isn't a lot of information about it. However, you can use this app for over 170 currencies, and it also works offline.

Easy Currency Converter

The Easy Currency Converter is rated number eight out of eleven apps on the list of currency converters. Through this app, you can get exchange rates for over 180 currencies that will automatically update if there is any change. On top of this, you can also get the exchange rate for four metals. This app will also let you check your history of exchange rates in order to better keep track of everything.

X Convert

The X Convert currency conversion has exchange rates for over 150 currencies. With this currency converter, you need to download rates, but this option is available offline. On top of the 150+ currencies, you can also get conversions for around 50 cryptocurrencies.

Amount

While you need to pay for this app, it only costs $0.99, and it is one of the best currency converters for Apple products. It not only made first place in the list of Converters, but is also in first place for currency converters for the Apple watch and fourth place in apps to convert measures. While your main goal is to find an app converter for currency, which Amount does, it's always nice to know you have a few extra tools available, such as converting measurements that also change with various countries. On top of this, it's one of the highest rated apps out there.

Of course, there are a lot more currency converters, so you might want to try a few before you decide on one. You might find that while you like some features on one, you might like other features on a different one. When it comes down to traveling to Ireland, either of these currency converters will work as they all have currency conversion for Euros and Sterling Pounds when exchanged from American dollars. However, because you will be traveling and Wi-Fi might not be available anywhere, you might want to find one that can work offline.

Chapter 10:

Places to Visit

With how beautiful Ireland is, there are tons of great places to see and visit. Ireland, which is basically an island, is surrounded by ocean. If you've never actually seen an ocean, Ireland would be a great place to see one for the first time.

Muckross House, Gardens, and Killarney National Park

The Muckross House and all that goes with it is typically the type of house you would see in movies or television shows, such as *Downton Abbey*. When you travel to Ireland, Muckross House and its gardens are a must-see. The house, which is part of Killarney National Park, is from the 19th century and it held some of the United Kingdom's royal family, such as Queen Victoria. At the time, this would have been one of the grandest affairs for Ireland. During the reign of Queen Victoria, people were honored to have the queen visit. However, the queen didn't visit people very often and she was known to be very selective of the places she stayed at.

The scenery around Muckross House makes it one of the most beautiful places to visit. On your drive and while you're there, you will see mountains and three lakes. Muckross House is the center point of Killarney National Park, and there definitely couldn't be a better centerpiece for Killarney.

If you've ever wanted to see a Victorian-style mansion, Muckross house is the place to see. It has been in Ireland's top places to see for years, and it doesn't seem like it'll change any time soon.

If you want to see Muckross House and gardens, the tour begins at around $70 and goes up, depending on what you decide to see and do. Many tourists who have seen the sites of Killarney National Park rave about the house and the tour guides as they are knowledgeable and know the complete history of the house and park.

Dublin

On the 2019 top ten list of must see places in Ireland, Dublin comes first. But this isn't the only list that Dublin is on, as it is also part of the Best Summer Vacations list, where it comes in at number four. Dublin also ranks fifth in Best Golf Destinations and number nine for Best Family Vacations in Europe. On top of this, Dublin also makes the list of Best Places to Visit in Europe at number 18. All these rankings come from The U.S. News & World Report for travel.[9]

9

    Dublin Travel Guide. Retrieved from https://travel.usnews.com/Dublin_Ireland/.

While this guide has already discussed Dublin a little, it's so iconic that there is so much to talk about. In fact, a travel guide could be written just about Dublin! This city is the largest in Ireland, and it continues to grow. When people move to Ireland, the majority of them head to Dublin. If not going directly to Dublin, most tourists make sure to still make it part of their trip.

Throughout the year, Dublin is host to dozens of festivals and other events. While Ireland is known for its year-round events, you could say the same for the city of Dublin. For example, from June through August, Dublin hosts the Irish Festival. They also have the Dublin LGBTQ Pride in June along with the Big Grill BBQ & Craft Beer Festival, which is held in August. From September through October, you can check out Dublin's Festival of History and their Theater Festival. Of course, Dublin also celebrates Oktoberfest. From December to January in Dublin, you can check out the New Year's Festival and the Dublin International Film Festival in February and March. Of course, Dublin takes part in a big St. Patrick's Day Festival, followed by the International Literature Festival in May.

On top of all these festivals, there are dozen of places to check out, from historic to cultural. For example, The Book of Kells and Trinity College is known to be the number one hot spot in Dublin, which was founded by Queen Elizabeth I in the early 1590s. Many people spend anywhere from a couple of hours to close to a half day visiting this tourist attraction.

One sight in Dublin that is often overlooked by tourists (and is FREE) is the Chester Beatty Library. This is a museum which holds documents dating back to 2700 B.C.

Of course, the Dublin Zoo and Phoenix Park are also highly popular places to visit in Dublin, and people typically spend about a half day to a full day here.

Galway

Galway is ranked as the third best place to visit by U.S. Travel News. Galway lays claim to the Cliffs of Moher and the Wild Atlantic Way. In Galway, it is best to walk around, which means that you don't have to worry about transportation. People say you should walk because there are many streets around Galway that are too small for vehicles. On top of this, there are many pedestrian only areas that you will want to check out. However, you can still use transportation buses as every town will offer tourist packages where you can take the bus to see some of the sites around the area.

Limerick

Like many other Irish cities, Limerick is big in keeping its tourists and residents busy. In Limerick, there are various festivals and events that you can visit throughout the year, along with many tourist destinations. Known as the first Irish City of Culture, Limerick has a lot of amazing architecture throughout the city. You also have a number of other places you can visit from the Limerick City Gallery of Art to St. Mary's Cathedral.

The Hunt Museum is another famous tourist destination spot in Limerick. The collection at this museum starts from the Neolithic era dating all the way to the last century. This museum was started by John and Gloria Hunt, who were antique collectors that donated their items to create this museum. Today, the museum is home to over 2,000 artifacts and documents.

On top of the museum, Limerick has its own pub so you can get a taste of pub culture in Ireland, and if you come at the right time of the year, you can also take part in one of Limerick's pub crawls. Another reason to visit Limerick is because of the art that fills the city's streets. Of course, there's also the food and the feel of Irish culture.

Kilkenny

Kilkenny, a castle that is over 400 years old, is one of the most exciting spots in Ireland. In Kilkenny, the most popular tourist destinations to visit are St. Frances Abbey, Rothe House, Black Abbey, Shee Alms House, and of course, Kilkenny Castle.

Kilkenny Castle was brought to life around the 1200s. Today, it is one of the most popular tourist attractions for many reasons. First, it is a piece of the history of Ireland. Second, although Kilkenny Castle has existed for a very long time, it is still one of the most well-kept historical buildings in Ireland. Additionally, other than seeing what the castle looked like in the 1200s, you can also see art from the National Art Gallery.

Cork

Cork is a city in the Republic of Ireland with a population of over 125,000, with many attractions for tourists.

Elizabeth Fort

The Elizabeth Fort was originally built around 1601, but it was then destroyed by the residents of Cork City. However, not too long after, it was rebuilt, but this time, the city's residents had to pay for it out of their own pocket. Of course, back in the early 1600s, they weren't happy. However, today, it is a different story, as the residents of Cork are incredibly proud of the Elizabeth Fort and enjoy showing it off to tourists.

St Fin Barre's Cathedral

While the St. Fin Barre's Cathedral was only built in the 1800s, the site the building stands on has held Cathedrals since the 7th century! Inside, the Cathedral is filled with amazing artwork and stained glass. And in good ol' fashioned Irish charm, the cathedral also holds a legend about an angel on the cathedral's east end. The legend states that this angel will blow into his bugle to announce the beginning of the Apocalypse.

University College Cork

If you want a walk to remember in Ireland, you'll want to visit the University College of Cork. Throughout your walk, you will see numerous sculptures and other works of art that will give you a taste of Ireland's culture, history, and art.

Cork Butter Museum

Food is not just a huge deal in Ireland, but also in Cork, home of the Cork Butter Museum. Because of Ireland's land and climate, it is known to have some of the best dairy products, from milk to butter. In this museum, there are exhibits where you can get a history lesson on butter in Ireland and take a walk through the exhibit showing you how butter was made in the past, and how it's made today.

Cork City Gaol

The Cork City Gaol gives tourists a great sense of historic architecture in Ireland. While at first glance, you might think it is a mansion or a castle, it's actually a jail. Of course, today, it's not used as a prison, but it shows how the cells used to look like back in the day. Historically, Cork City Gaol was mainly a women's prison, and it housed Republicans during the War of Independence.

Aran Islands

The Aran Islands are one of the most beautiful sights you will find in all of Ireland. They are located along the Wild Atlantic Way, not too far from the cities of Doolin and Galway. The Aran Islands are placed on top of a 300 foot cliff known as the Dun Aonghasa. The Aran Islands are made up of 3 islands. The first island, which is the largest one, is called the Inis Mor Island. Inis Meain Island is the second largest island. It is located right next to Inis Mor Island and has a population of about 200 people. Inis Oirr Island is the third and smallest island, and it is located right next to Inis Meain Island.

Antrim, Northern Ireland

Antrim makes up one of the six counties of Northern Ireland. It's home to many beautiful sights, such as the Giant's Causeway, the Dunluce Castle, the Carrickfergus Castle, and it has ties to the popular TV show *Game of Thrones*.

2019 Open Championship will be held here

On July 18-21, 2019, the 148th Opening Championship will be held in Antrim, Northern Ireland, at the Royal Portrush. During this time, Antrim will be buzzing with activity as this is the first time since 1951 that they've held the Opening Championship for Golf. While the tickets for the 2019 Open Championship have already sold out, you can still purchase practice day tickets.

Ballintoy Harbour filming location for Iron Islands in "Game of Thrones."

If you're a *Game of Thrones* fan, you have to go to Antrim in Northern Ireland on your vacation, where you can take a tour of Ballintoy Harbour, which was one of the filming locations for the show. Ballintoy Harbour was used to film shots of Iron Islands and the exterior Pyke shots. In fact, if you are a huge *Game of Throne* fan, there will be an exhibit focusing on the TV show in Antrim through several months in 2019. The exhibit will be located at the TEC Belfast from April 11th all the way to September 1st. If you want more information, such as how to get tickets, head to discovernorthernireland.com.[10]

Giant's Causeway

The Giant's Causeway is home to the iconic hexagonal stones, which were created by a volcanic eruption. This historic and amazing landmark is located only a few miles from Bushmills, a little village of around 1,000 people.

---

[10] GAME OF THRONES™: The Touring Exhibition, Belfast. Retrieved from https://discovernorthernireland.com/GAME-OF-THRONES-The-Touring-Exhibition-Belfast-P78087/?s=1C46D3E9DBD1FE1B279165B1082C8545748ECE8E.

Of course, there is no way you will go to Ireland without hearing about the myth behind the construction of the Giant's Causeway. The myth goes that Irish giant Fionn mac Cumhaill and Scottish giant, Benandonner were set to meet at that location for a fight. After accepting the challenge to fight, Fionn built the Causeway directly across the northern channel. With the Causeway built, the two giants could then officially meet. There are two endings to the myth. One goes that Fionn defeated Benandonner, and the second claims that Fionn hid from Benandonner because Fionn was much smaller than him.

Dunluce Castle

In Antrim, Northern Ireland, there are so many sights to see. You absolutely don't want to miss the sunset behind the Dunluce Castle. Of course, seeing any castle in Ireland is amazing, (and there are so many!) but the view with the sunset is just spectacular. You don't want to get too close to the Dunluce Castle, as it's falling apart and is unsafe. For instance, the castle no longer has its kitchen because it fell into the water. With Dunluce Castle being located next to a cliff, the castle is slowly losing some of its pieces. However, none of this takes away from the beauty of the sunset. In fact, many people who have seen the iconic sunset only believe the slowly vanishing castle makes the scene more breathtaking and mysterious.

Carrickfergus Castle

Carrickfergus Castle in Antrim, Northern Ireland is one of the many castles in Ireland that you can explore. With this castle standing for over 800 years, you will hear many stories while taking a tour of the castle. If you're interested in medieval life, this is definitely a castle you will want to see. This castle, one of the most well-documented in Ireland, allows you to see how people in medieval times lived.

Landscapes

Just like other areas in Ireland, the landscapes that make up County Antrim, Northern Ireland are some of the most breathtaking scenes you will ever come across in your life. When you visit, you will want to make sure to bring comfortable shoes or maybe even hiking shoes as you will walk a lot, all while admiring the beautiful scenery. You'll be able to walk up and down the hills, stand on the cliffs and look at the Atlantic Ocean, or stand on a hill and look down towards a city or farmhouses.

Glens of Antrim

Glens of Antrim makes up a large part of County Antrim in Northern Ireland. As you walk and take in the landscape, you're sure to find a few, if not all, of the nine Glens of Antrim. The names of these nine Glens of Antrim are:

1. Glenballyemon
2. Glencloy
3. Glendun
4. Glenariff
5. Glenarm
6. Glanaan
7. Glenshesk
8. Glencorp
9. Glentaisie

Just like every other part of Ireland, the Glens of Antrim are known to host their own festivals and days of celebration throughout the year. If you're able to catch one of these celebrations, you will get a taste of some of Ireland's famous foods and drinks, witnessing Irish culture first hand. You'll also be able to listen and take in Irish music. You'll hear different instruments played on stage and see the different steps from the Irish dancers. With each step they take on stage, you'll be able to hear the clicks of their special shoes. You'll also be able to witness the special outfits made for the dancers.

Chapter 11:

Tours You Should Go On

When you travel to Ireland, there are dozens of tours where you will learn an incredible amount of history about Ireland. You'll also be able to see and get a taste of Ireland's culture. On top of this, you'll be able to see dozens of amazing, beautiful sights that you'll never forget.

Best of Ireland Tour

The Best of Ireland Tour is one of the most popular tours in Ireland. It lasts eight nights and starts the moment you reach the island. This tour has a set itinerary which will tell you exactly where you'll be from one day to the next and what you'll be learning, doing, and where you'll be traveling. When you get your eight day schedule, it'll be very detailed. Below is an example of what your schedule will look like, but it is more like a summary. When you receive the actual schedule, it'll have a lot more information than this.

Day 1: Dublin to Kilkenny

After you receive your rental car, you will head to the National Stud and Japanese Gardens. At the National Stud museum, you'll receive a history of horse racing. The Japanese Gardens are in the same area but will give you a different Irish history as the Japanese Gardens don't focus on horse racing. The Japanese Gardens were established in the early 1900s and show the life of a human being from the time of their birth to the time of their death.

After you finish your tour at the Japanese Gardens, you'll head to the old Irish city of Kilkenny. In Kilkenny, you'll find history dating back thousands of years. Of course, Kilkenny Castle will be one of the big stops. You'll also want to make sure to check out Saint Canice's Cathedral, which will give you a glimpse of architecture from the 13th century.

Day 2: Kilkenny to Kinsale, County Cork

On your second day of the eight day tour, you will leave the city of Kilkenny and continue your journey to Kinsale. On your second day, the first place you will visit is the Rock of Cashel, an area where St. Patrick is believed to have spoken. In addition, it's an area where several kings throughout history have spent time. The Rock of Cashel is very rich in history.

After the Rock of Cashel, you will check out the Cobh Heritage Center. Here, you'll learn Irish history, such as the port of Cobh, the last port where anyone heard anything from the Titanic ship in 1912. It's believed that the last call the captain made before the Titanic hit the iceberg was done to this port.

After your trip to Cobh, you will head to the Irish city of Kinsal. In this city, you'll be able to see the International Museum of Wine, where you'll hear a dozen romantic stories and the history of how the wine trade helped Ireland become what it is today.

Day 3: Kinsale to Killarney

On the third day of the eight day tour, you will visit Blarney Castle and drive a longer route from Kinsale to Killarney. Along this route, you will see dozens of landmarks, rolling hills, and other examples of beautiful Irish landscape. Also, you will get to see the Bantry House and its Gardens. Along your drive, you will come across the Caha Mountains, which is one of the most breathtaking scenes of day three.

Once you get to Killarney, you will see the castle and Killarney National Park. This park is different from many other parks in Ireland as it is science-related. Of course, around Killarney, you will see many other things such as the Ross Castle as you take a walk and check out the landscapes.

Day 4: Killarney, the Ring of Kerry, and Muckross House

Your fourth day of the eight day tour is filled with even more breathtaking sights, so you will want to make sure you have your camera ready to take some amazing photographs. In day four, there are a variety of touring options, and you will probably not be able to fit them all into one day. However, this just means you'll need to make a list of the sights you didn't see and make another trip to Ireland!

You can start your driving tour by visiting the Ring of Kerry. Like with most sights in Ireland, you will be taken aback by the scenery and will probably want to take pictures to show your family back home why they have to plan their own trip to Ireland and see these amazing sights. As you drive along the Ring of Kerry, you will find your way to Muckross House, an amazing, popular Victorian mansion.

Day 5: Killarney to Galway

On your fifth day of the eight day tour, you will leave Killarney and head to Galway. While we've already discussed Galway a little, there are still many more sights to see there. Of course, before you actually reach Galway, you will have other sights to view, such as the Village of Adare, which is believed to be one of the most beautiful villages in Ireland. On top of this, you will also want to see the ancient church of the Village of Adare.

On day five, you will visit the Bunratty Castle, which has been standing since the early 1400s. Of course, you can also visit King John's Castle. However, you won't want to spend too much time at the castles because you absolutely can't miss out on the famous Cliffs of Moher. This is another sight this travel guide has discussed, and it is known to be one of the greatest sights of Ireland as you stand on the cliff and look over the Atlantic Ocean. If you've never seen an ocean, this is one of the best ways to see one for the first time. Even if you've seen an ocean before, you won't want to miss the view of the Atlantic Ocean from the Cliffs of Moher.

At the end of the fifth day, you will arrive in Galway. Of course, it'll be a bit late, so you might be tired. However, don't let this bother you as on the sixth day of the tour, you will spend your day in Galway.

Day 6: Galway and the Connemara Region

On the sixth day of the trip, you will spend the day touring the many sights of Galway and the surrounding area. One of the main things you will want to see is the Connemara Region, with some more amazing instances of Ireland scenery. Before you head to Connemara, you will want to make sure that you have enough space on your camera's memory card and batteries because you will be taking a lot of amazing photographs. On the top of the mountains, you will also be able to see amazing rivers and a beautiful coastline.

In the Connemara Region, you will be able to check out the sights of Kylemore Abbey, Sky Road, and the Village of Roundstone, which is known to be one of the best villages for fishing. While you're checking out the sights of Galway, you can take the Ferry to the Aran Islands before heading back to your accommodation and getting a taste of Ireland's nightlife. This is a great opportunity to check out a pub in Galway, listen to some live music, and have a proper Irish meal.

Day 7: Galway to Dublin

On the seventh day of your eight day journey, you will leave Galway and head back towards Dublin, but not on the same route that you came from. Instead, you will head to Dublin via the Clonmacnoise, an ancient Irish settlement. Founded in the 6th century, this is some of the oldest Irish history on the tour. You will also get to see Christian grave slabs, large crosses, and round towers.

In this part of the trip, you will have the choice between different sights, such as Kilmainham Gaol, Guinness Storehouse, the National Museum of Ireland, Trinity Castle and the Book of Kells, Dublin Castle, and many other sights. Of course, you won't be able to see all of these in one day, so you will have to pick which ones you want to see and which ones you will leave for the next time you are in Ireland. At the end of the day, you will reach Dublin. Once you arrive, you can decide to check out the nightlife or just head back to your hotel.

Day 8: Dublin and its Many Sights to See

This is the last day of your eight day tour, which will be spent going around Dublin and checking out as many sights as you possibly can. Of course, Dublin has so much history and attractions that it's impossible to discuss them all in this tourist guide. Some great attractions in Dublin include the James Joyce Center, Christ Church Cathedral, and the Dublin Writers Museum. Of course, you will want to take some time to eat at a Dublin restaurant for lunch before checking out the many other sites throughout the day. If you're not sure what to order, try the Irish stew, one of the most famous Irish dishes.

Also, if you've never checked out the Dublin nightlife, now is the time. Dublin is home to some of the most amazing pubs, which is a good place to stop and eat your evening meal. Once you find a good pub, you can learn some more about Irish history and culture as there will be many waiters and waitresses on hand. You will find that many of them are all too happy to talk to you about your Irish experience and answer any questions you might have.

Day 9: End of Your Tour

Today, your tour of Ireland is officially over, and you will have to check out of your hotel room and head home. However, perhaps you may decide to spend a few more days in Ireland as there is probably still a lot you haven't been able to see!

Cliffs of Moher Tour

The Cliffs of Moher tour is another fantastic tour that you can take during your visit to Ireland. Of course, if you take the eight day tour, you will be able to see the Cliffs of Moher, but you won't be able to take the special tour for it.

While the Cliffs of Moher is definitely a sight to see, in the tour, you will go deeper and learn about the history of the Cliffs of Moher and hear stories that you won't hear anywhere else. And these are not stories you'll want to miss! You won't want to focus too much on the maps of the Cliff of Moher as this will make you miss the beautiful scenery surrounding the cliffs and part of the Wild Atlantic Way. Because the Cliffs of Moher is part of the 1,000 miles of the Wild Atlantic Way, you'll be able to see a beautiful piece of it. The Wild Atlantic Way is a popular tourist attraction, but because it's about 1,000 miles long, people aren't able to see the whole attraction. Therefore, travellers often check out smaller tourist attractions within the Wild Atlantic Way, such as the Cliffs of Moher.

Many people suggest that if you want to see the Cliffs of Moher, you should take this tour because the roads are difficult to navigate, especially if you've never been there before. In the tour, you will be able to soak up all the information and the scenery while an experienced driver takes you along the road.

The Cliffs of Moher Tour is about 13 hours long, and your tour guide will pick you up at a central location in Dublin. While you're heading to the Cliffs of Moher, you'll be able to see the Bunratty Castle and Lahinch, which is a village on the way to the Cliffs of Moher. After you spend a good part of the day at the Cliffs, you'll head back to Dublin. However, before you return to Dublin, you will pass by Galway and make a stop, where you will do a half hour walking tour.

Game of Thrones Tours

The Game of Thrones Tours is another full day tour, which takes a total of 11 hours. While it is a long day, you will love the sights and stops that this tour has to offer, especially if you're a big fan of the show. By creating the Game of Thrones Tour, Ireland has worked to keep the legacy of the TV show alive in their culture. Also, as we've previously discussed, they're opening up a new Game of Thrones exhibit. This is something you definitely want to check out if you're a die hard Game of Thrones fan! The exhibit will showcase the TV show with costumes worn by the actors!

You will leave from the Hilton Garden Inn, Dublin, at 8:00 am. Before you take this tour, you will be given an overview of its schedule. This schedule not only lists the stops and the sights you will see, but also tells you how long you will have for each stop. For example, your first stop is Tollymore Forest Park. You will get here at 10:15 and you will spend about an hour and a half walking through Tollymore Forest Park. Also, on this tour, you will get to see Strangford Lough, Inch Abbey, and Castle Ward.

Cork Ghost Tour

If you're interested in ghost stories, then you should definitely check out the Cork Ghost Tour! In this tour, located in Cork, Ireland, you will walk around and hear ghost stories about Cork, and there will even be actors in costume to help tell these stories. This tour only takes a couple of hours, but it is rated as one of the best tours. Also, you can take your children on this tour if you want to. While the stories can be a bit scary, they're also very fun and factual. While listening to the stories, you'll receive a history lesson of the city of Cork.

Castle Tours

There are so many castles around Ireland, and you are able to tour many of them. Here are a few you could add to your list!

Trim Castle

Trim Castle is located in Trim, Ireland and is run similar to a museum. They are open throughout the week, usually from about 9:30 am to 5:30 pm. Keep in mind that this tour might close during the winter, so you will want to make sure to check out their live hours before heading there. Once you get there, you will get to see the castle while you're given a guided tour. This tour takes about two to three hours to complete.

Ross Castle

Ross Castle is located in Killarney, Ireland and, like Trim Castle, limits its hours or closes for the winter season. By taking a guided tour through Ross Castle, you'll not only learn of its history, as it was built in the 15th Century, but also hear the story of the ghost who still roams the halls of Ross Castle. So, if you're fascinated with ghosts, this is another great tour you won't want to miss.

Dublin Castle

You can also take a guided castle tour at the 13th Century Dublin Castle. Here, you can learn about the Irish government's history, who still use Dublin Castle to this day. This tour lasts one to two hours.

Malahide Castle

Malahide Castle, an amazing 12th century castle, is not too far from Dublin, and you can also take a guided tour of it. This guided tour is about two to three hours long, with a 45 minute section on the history of the Talbot family who owned the castle for around 800 years.

Pub Tours

Pubs tours are a great way to learn an important part of Irish culture. Like castle tours, there are many pub tours you can go on during your time in Ireland.

Rural Pub Tours

On the Rural Pub Tour, you will go from pub to pub, which will allow you to see some of Ireland's scenery as well as get a taste of their culture. The great thing about this tour is that none of them are in the city, so you will get to see breathtaking scenes from the Irish countryside. As you go from one pub to the next, you will pass by dozens of farms. Also, you'll be taken to some pubs that you don't hear much about because they tend to be hidden within the rolling hills of the countryside. This tour is estimated to take three hours or more.

Connemara Pub Tours

The Connemara Pub Tour focuses on pubs in the Connemara region. The duration of this tour is around three hours, and it gives you a glimpse of Irish culture's pub nightlife. One of the great things about this pub tour is that food and drink are offered for a discount since you're part of the Connemara Pub Tour.

Irish Pub Tour

The Irish Pub Tour is an 8 to 9 day tour in Dublin. The tour starts at 2 in the afternoon in Dublin. First, you will meet at your hotel and take a tour around Dublin on a tourist bus. You will then make a stop at the Guinness Storehouse where you will learn how Guinness makes its beer. After the tour, you will also actually be able to taste the beer!

On the second day, you will visit Glasnevin Cemetery Museum, where you can learn about dozens of people in Ireland's history. You will also stop at the Smithwick's Experience brewery. Of course, you won't want to miss out on Kilkenny's historic pubs and walking tour!

On the third day of the tour, you will visit the sites of the House of Waterford Crystal and Blarney Castle. Of course, you will also be able to check out a variety of pubs in Killarney. This is the perfect time to check out Ireland's nightlife!

On the fourth day, you will visit Kate Kearney's Cottage and the Dingle Peninsula. When you visit Dingle Peninsula, you will not only be able to see amazing Ireland scenery, but you will also be able to see the filming location for *Far & Away*, a 1992 romantic drama movie and *Ryan's Daughter,* a drama movie from 1970. After you spend the day touring the city of Dingle, you can have your evening meal at Kate Kearney's Cottage before checking out some night time entertainment in Ireland.

On the fifth day, you will visit the Aillwee Cave and the Cliffs of Moher. At the Cliffs of Moher, you will be able to walk along the cliffs and take in the Atlantic coast scenery. From there, you will stop at McGann's Pub before heading to the Aillwee Caves. Finally, you will take a stop at Johnny Burke's Pub, which is located in the hotel you will be staying at that evening.

Westport Walk and Galway are the two major tourist attractions for the sixth day. Galway is a city close to the sea, so you will be able to take in the scenery before checking out the city. In the afternoon, you will travel to Westport, where you will go on a pub walking tour.

On the seventh day, as you head back to Dublin, you will check out the Teeling Distillery and the 12th Century Brazen Head Pub. This will be your last night in the hotel, so if you haven't checked out Ireland's nightlife yet, now is the time to do it! Remember, a big part of the Irish culture is the nightlife, which is filled with music and great pub food!

Dublin Traditional Irish Music Pub Crawl

There are a variety of pubs in Dublin, Ireland. In fact, there are over 700 pubs located in the city of Dublin! While you might not be able to visit all the pubs in Dublin during your vacation, you can visit as many as possible through one of Dublin's pub crawls.

Within the Dublin Traditional Irish Music Pub Crawl, there are two different tours you can choose from. The first tour is the Music Pub Crawl. This tour is priced starting at $18.30 with a starting time of 7:30. The second tour is called the Pub Crawl with Dinner Show and starts at 6:00 pm. This tour holds a price tag starting at $54.89.

For this tour, if you chose the dinner, you will head to Flanagan's where you will eat your three course meal before you head over to Temple Bar. The tour guides for this pub crawl are two local musicians from the Dublin area. Everyone will meet in Temple Bar at 7:30 pm and then walk from one pub to the next in order to take part of Ireland's nightlife.

This tour takes about two and a half hours and includes private seating at all the pubs you visit.

Chapter 12:

Attractions to Behold

The one thing this guide cannot discuss enough are the amazing attractions on the island of Ireland. Whether you're traveling to Northern Ireland or the Republic of Ireland, you will get to see plenty of amazing attractions. Unfortunately, unless you're staying for a long time, you're going to have a tough time seeing them all, but it's definitely worth seeing as many of them as you can.

In this chapter, you will notice that we will speak about some attractions that we have already previously discussed in other chapters, and we've done this for a couple of reasons. First, these attractions are so full of beauty and have such amazing scenery that they are definitely among the top places to see in Ireland. Second, there is so much information you can learn about these attractions before you even set foot on Irish soil that it helps to put them in multiple spots of this guide. And, of course, one of the reasons is because of their beauty and the amount of information you learn at the attraction. I mean, it's pretty hard to stop talking about the Cliffs of Moher! While you can get a sense of their beauty through the many pictures in this travel guide, (and so many more on the internet) the pictures will never compare to seeing them in real life.

As I have previously mentioned, it's impossible to talk about everything Ireland holds in just one guide. However,

I will talk about a few iconic attractions that are on many must-see lists you can find online.

Cliffs of Moher

Because this travel guide has already spoken about the Cliffs of Moher, we won't discuss it in too much detail here. The Cliffs of Moher are located in Liscannor, Ireland. You can take a guided tour of the Cliffs of Moher, which should take 2 to 3 hours. Here, you will see 700 feet tall cliffs looking out towards the Atlantic Ocean. Also, the Cliffs of Moher have their own visitors center where you can get more information and even buy some souvenirs. If it's around meal time, you can also check out one of the two cafes located along the cliffs. Of course, if you really want to, you can check out both, and maybe even have a meal at one and your dessert at the other cafe!

Ring of Kerry

Ring of Kerry is located in County Kerry, Ireland, and is one of the most beautiful sights of County Kerry. Of course, County Kerry holds many more amazing sights to see, but Ring of Kerry is an absolute must-see. At the Ring of Kerry, there are a few different tours that you can take. For example, you could take the bus, with most of the tours running all day, so you will see more than just the Ring of Kerry. However, the Ring of Kerry also holds its own tour, which is about 2 to 3 hours long.

The Ring of Kerry is part of the Wild Atlantic Way and is a beauty like no other in County Kerry. Also, aside from the beautiful sights, you can play golf, water ski, and fish. As many people say after they visit County Kerry, it is "a once in a lifetime experience."[11]

Rock of Cashel

The Rock of Cashel in Cashel, County Tipperary, Ireland is one of the most amazing sights and one of the most popular attractions for tourists. Here, you can join a guided tour of the 13th Century Cathedral. The tour lasts around 1 to 2 hours and is a great way to get learn some history and stories of the sight. This stunning location is on top of a hill which you can see for miles as you start to drive up. The Rock of Cashel is complete with a round tower and sturdy walls that encircle the whole building.

Guinness Storehouse

Of course, the Guinness Storehouse is another amazing sight to see. Guinness is one of Ireland's most iconic beers and by taking a tour of the Guinness Storehouse, you can

---

[11] Ring of Kerry Tourism Co Kerry Ireland. (2019). Retrieved from https://ringofkerrytourism.com/.

see how the beer is produced, get a behind the scenes look of what it takes to get all the pints to Ireland's pubs and stores and other places in the world. Of course, after the whole process, you can also get a taste of Guinness. Located at the St. James's Gate Brewery in Dublin, the Guinness Storehouse first saw the light of day in 1759, with the establishment of Guinness brewery. At the time, its founder Arthur Guinness signed a lease for the building that lasts 9,000 years!

Dunluce Castle

Dunluce Castle is located in Northern Ireland near Portrush and along the Causeway Coast. While this is another one of Ireland's large and beautiful castles, it's tucked away in a way that you might not see it at first. Dunluce Castle is located right along a cliff, but is still accessible to people of all ages. When you view Dunluce Castle, you also get an amazing view of the ocean. Both of these sights together can make for one of the greatest pictures you can take in Ireland.

Chapter 13:

Safety in Ireland

Whenever a person travels, safety is always one of their main concerns, not because of crime rates, but just because you never know what can happen. Of course, age is always a factor in this. If you're elderly, you're going to worry about something happening to your health more than someone younger. If you're a parent and you're bringing your children, you're going to be concerned about their safety. You're not just going to be concerned about the crime rate in Ireland but you're also going to be concerned about their safety at many sites you want them to see. Of course, some of the tours available to you may seem a bit more dangerous for children than others. For example, Dunluce Castle, which is on the edge of a cliff, will seem like a very dangerous place for children. However, rest assured, Ireland has already taken care of this! Ireland realizes that they are one of the hottest tourist spots and they handle this with pride and make sure their sights are safe for everyone. Of course, you want to make sure to do your parental duty and keep an eye on your children.

Medication

First thing's first, before you go touring Ireland, you want to make sure you're safe. For example, if you take medication, you want to make sure you're going to have enough of it for your whole journey. You're also going to want to talk to your pharmacist or doctor to ensure you have a solid backup plan. The reason for this is because while you may have enough pills, things happen and they could easily get lost or stolen. Therefore, you want to make sure you know what steps to take in Ireland in case you urgently need a refill. It also never hurts to create your own mini first aid kit to bring with you on your trip. This is one of the items on the list in the "what to pack" chapter in this travel guide. However, it doesn't hurt to say this again - pack your own small first aid kit, and it doesn't hurt to carry it with you wherever you go!

Emergency Numbers

You might also want to create a list of emergency numbers. While we tend to keep all our numbers in our phones, people in Ireland won't know who your family members are. Furthermore, in order to protect what's on your phone, it's important to have a code so people can't randomly open it up and check out all your information. The downside to having a lock on your phone's home screen is that emergency personnel won't be able to get ahold of your family if something happened to you.

Therefore, it's just best to write down your emergency contact information on a sheet of paper and carry it with you in your wallet or pocket. This way, if you ever find yourself in an emergency where you can't tell the emergency personnel who you are and who to contact, they have the information right there. And trust me, if something happens and they need to know who you are, they will look for your passport or another form of ID, so it's a good idea to keep it along with that.

Also, on your list, you could add the phone numbers for local law enforcement in Ireland. Of course, they are always close to any public attractions, but you never know what the future holds, so it's always a good idea to be extra prepared in case you need to call the local police in Ireland. To give you a little information about Ireland's police service, they are known as the Gardai in the Republic of Ireland. In Northern Ireland, they are referred to as the PSNI or the Police Service of Northern Ireland. They can both be reached by dialing 112 or 999 from your phone in Ireland. This is basically like 911 in the United States. If you want to know what other emergency numbers you should keep on your list, you could keep the contact number of anyone who works at the visitors center in the areas you're visiting.

Crime in Ireland

Of course, when people look at the safety of a country or area they are about to travel to, they usually turn to crime rates first. However, there is a lot more information than that that people should know. First, for your own safety, it is always a good idea to research the areas you are going to. Chances are, like most people who go on vacation, you're going to have your schedule set before you take the plane to Ireland. This means that before you even leave the comfort of your home, you can take the time to check out each area you're going to and research their crime rates. All this information is available online. This will allow you to prepare yourself to ensure that not only you but everyone you're traveling with is prepared for the types of crime that take place in that area.

Having said that, it's important to note that you can't avoid crime. Think about it - crime is everywhere. It's even near where you live. No matter where you go, there will always be some type of crime. The trick is to do your research and be prepared so you can protect yourself, your family, those you're traveling with, and your possessions. On top of this, the most important piece of information is to not go on a trip overly worried about crime. While you might find places, such as dark alleys that you want to avoid (especially at night), you don't want these worries to ruin your amazing vacation. The thing about Ireland is that every single sight you see is going to make you forget about any crime. Anyway, Ireland doesn't have a high crime rate to begin with. However, this doesn't mean that they don't have any crime. Like every other location in the world, they do, and all it takes to stay safe is to do some research and read the tips below so you can avoid being the target of a crime while on vacation.

Bag snatchers and Pickpocketers

People who pick pockets and snatch bags and run always hang out around the hottest tourist crowds. So, while in those areas, watch out for these thieves. These criminals can be some of the most strategic criminals you find because they are aware that they're in a large crowd, and they use it as cover.

One of the biggest reasons you want to try to avoid looking like a tourist is because bag snatchers and pickpocketers target them. They know that tourists aren't going to pay as much attention to the people around them because they're just taking in the scenery (and this is something that will be 100% true when you visit Ireland). Therefore, make sure to be aware of the people around you.

Pickpocketers will often target people who have pockets on the back as they are easier targets. However, they don't just pay attention to pockets, as they also observe purses. They are often pros at being able to take something out of a pocket or out of a purse without you feeling a thing. Some people believe that as long as they have their bag zipped up, they will be able to feel someone trying to unzip their bag. Wrong! Professional pickpocketers already know how to unzip a bag without you knowing, especially if you're wearing a backpack or if your purse isn't directly under your arm. This is why, when it comes to traveling, while they are easy to carry, you want to stay away from backpacks. You also want to make sure your purse is zipped and closed up as tight as possible and to keep your purse securely under your arm. This will make it much harder for pickpocketers to get to your valuable items, money, or credit cards, so you will be less likely to be a target. The thing with pickpocketers is that they don't want to spend much time on one person because they don't have the time. They have to be quick and make their move in order not to look suspicious and get caught.

Bag snatchers are criminals who grab your bag and run off as quickly as they can. They usually have an escape route, so they know exactly where to run to. However, when they are snatching a bag from a large crowd, it's also easy for them to get lost in it. And no matter how much you yell for someone in front of you to stop them, people usually have slow reactions, which means that the bag snatcher can often easily outrun them. I am not trying to say that people don't care or don't want to help, it's just how it works when someone says something and how long it takes for the other person's brain to register this. Again, one of the best ways to not make yourself a target is to securely hold your purse and bag underneath your arm and make sure you have your hand on it at all times.

Other than the precautions we've already discussed with pickpockets and bag snatchers, you can also do other things to keep yourself from becoming a target for these types of criminals. For example, it is a good idea not to wear any valuables. While we will want to wear our wedding rings, it's OK to leave your valuables locked up safely at home. Another tip is to wear your bags across your body and not on your shoulder. This will make it harder for both types of criminals, but especially bag snatchers. They want to be able to make a quick escape, so they won't aim for a person who has a bag strapped across their body. Another tip is to not leave your bag loosely lying around a table in a restaurant. Try to keep the strap of the bag on your leg, leave the bag on your lap, or fasten the bag to your chair in some way. If you're in a booth, make sure your bag is near a corner and keep the strap around your arm or around your body. Furthermore, never leave your possessions unattended. Don't even leave them in your rental car or in the hotel as when you're not around, you never know what could happen.

Sexual Assault or Robbery

The tricks that you probably learned in elementary school, high school, or college can be used to avoid a robbery or sexual assault when you're in another country. For example, don't walk down dark alleys or quiet streets, whether at night or during the day. When traveling, you always want to do what you can to remain in a group or use the buddy system. Do your best to make sure you're not alone, and remember to lock your hotel room or other accommodation whenever you leave. Many people don't always think of locking their hotel room doors and while most of them lock automatically these days, it's always possible that the door didn't securely fasten, which means that it could still be open, making you susceptible to an attack.

While people don't often hear about robberies on the street anymore, they still happen, so be aware of your surroundings. Of course, it helps to remain close to other people and crowds. One of the first rules is literally to give the robber what they want. While we automatically want to fight to keep our items, especially our passports, money, and other valuables we carry in our purse or wallet, you're less likely to have to face bodily harm if you give the robber what they ask for. On top of this, don't flash any of your personal items. If you're wearing your large diamond ring, do what you can to make sure it's covered up to help keep you safe from an attack of any sort.

While you can't always stay clear of sexual assault, you can help reduce your chances of becoming a victim. For example, stay out of quiet and dark streets at night, especially the alleys. Of course, you don't want to go down them during the day either as sexual assault can happen at any time. You also want to make sure that you're not getting drunk, not taking drugs (except for your prescription medication), and not going to parties unless you are accompanied by someone else. In addition, you should remain close to the person or people you're with. Of course, you also want to avoid taking part in hitchhiking as this can easily lead to attacks.

Credit Card, Fraud, and Scams

No matter where you are in the world, you can become a victim of credit card fraud and scams. Unfortunately, just like in other places in the world, these types of crimes are on the rise in Ireland. One of the best ways to avoid this is to be aware of your surroundings. If you have to pay with your card, always keep your eye on it and don't leave your pin number anywhere near it. Also, if you notice people acting suspiciously around the ATM, don't go there. Just find a different ATM. If people are acting strange around an ATM, they could be preparing to scam the numbers from the next person who uses it.

Know the prices of the souvenirs you're paying for and make sure you are not getting ripped off. Unfortunately, this crime generally happens a lot in tourist areas, including in Ireland. The only reason this could qualify as a scam is if the item is marked up at the register and you don't pay for it right away. For example, if you are purchasing a souvenir that is 20 Euros but when you get to the register it's been marked up to 30, tell them, as they might be trying to scam you. If you pay for the item and realize you overpaid, you've lost your money and can't catch the person anymore.

Again, it's important to stress not to be too paranoid about crime. First, Ireland is very aware of the heavy tourist traffic, and they try their best to make sure every tourist has a safe vacation in Ireland. Yes, they want you to see the sights, but they also want you to come back! They love the company of tourists and do anything they can to make sure you have a great trip. Second, every place in the world deals with crime. Wherever you are, don't let crime ruin your vacation. Three, if you're cautious and use the tips given, you are less likely to be a target. Just like wherever you are in this world, including the grocery store and restaurant by your house, you could become a target of a random crime, especially if you're unaware of your surroundings or don't take care of your possessions. Also, don't forget to have a list of emergency phone numbers just in case you need to dial 211, 999, or if something happens to you and someone needs to contact your family.

Conclusion

By reading this travel guide, you've learned about so many of Ireland's great adventures. You've not only learned what your trip could cost and what to pack, but also how to handle Ireland's quirky weather. You now know all about places to visit, things to see, and even some fun facts about Ireland.

This travel guide is not only for people who have decided to visit Ireland but also for those of you who are still deciding. Hopefully, if successful, this guide will have convinced you to someday take a trip to this beautiful and majestic country.

In this travel guide, we have spoken about some of the most beautiful and popular destinations, all of which are on the list of must-sees for many travelers heading to Ireland. Remember, Ireland started its history thousands of years ago, which means that it's full of ancient sights and landmarks that you won't be able to see anywhere else. Some of the beautiful attractions you can visit include Giant's Causeway, Guinness Storehouse, Dunluce Castle, Ring of Kerry, and Rock of Cashel.

On top of the attractions, you won't want to miss some of the most popular tours such as the Game of the Thrones Tours, the Cork Ghost Tour, the Cliffs of Moher Tours, and the Castle Tours. Plus, if you've never seen a castle or been on a cruise, now's your chance. In fact, some of the best cruises Ireland has to offer will have stops at a few castles!

In closing, everyone should visit Ireland at least once in their life. Of course, once you go to Ireland, you're going to want to go back! No matter what time of the year you decide to go, you're going to be busy with the various sites throughout the island, and there are events happening every month to help you get a better taste of Irish culture.

Bonus Chapter:

Little Known Irish Facts

Now, it's time to get down to the bonus chapter of this travel guide, the little known Irish Facts! When you're in Ireland and taking in all the sights you can, you're going to hear a lot of stories, myths, facts, and legends as this is a large part of Ireland's culture. You can always take part in this by remembering some of your own little Irish facts taken right from this travel guide!

1. We all know that Ireland is big for its beer. It loves its Guinness and Irish people are not shy about this. But did you know that Irish people are only the sixth biggest drinkers in the world? As it's been said before, Ireland loves its beer, and now you understand how true this is. In fact, the average person in Ireland drinks about 100 liters of beer annually.

2. But just because Irish people like to drink a lot, it doesn't mean they can take home the trophy of biggest Guinness drinkers, as Nigeria drinks more of it than the Irish, who are the ones who make it!

3. The famous Saint Patrick was not actually Irish. Even though Ireland holds the life of Saint Patrick with high esteem and celebrates Saint Patrick annually, he was kidnapped by Irish pirates and wasn't even born in Ireland. However, Saint Patrick

returned to Ireland, where he focused on changing Ireland's history forever.

4. Ireland is known for its beautiful landscapes and amazing attractions, many of which you were introduced to in this travel guide. But did you know that Ireland is also famous for having a city with an extremely long name? The name of the city is Muckanaghederdauhaulia (yes, try saying that one), and it's a small city located in the County of Galway. Try to see if you can find this small city with the long name when you're touring the County of Galway!

5. Did you know that 10 million pints of Guinness can be produced on a typical business day? Just another reason to check out the amazing Guinness Storehouse! I wonder if they have a daily record they keep track of?

6. Ireland is known for many things, from its exciting tourist attractions to producing millions of pints of Guinness annually. They are also known for their leprechauns and Shamrocks. And you probably also think they are well-known for their redheads. However, in reality, only 9% of Ireland has red hair!

7. You know England is known for its tea. However, Ireland is the third highest tea consumer, and drinks more tea than England!

8. Ireland is home to Europe's fourth largest stadium! When you travel to Dublin, you will have to make sure you take a trip to Croke Park as this grandiose stadium has the capacity to hold up to 82,300

people. Several sports games are held in Croke Park, such as soccer and football. Today, it is run by the Gaelic Games Association.

9. The first submarine used by the United States Navy was invented by an Irish lad called John Philip Holland.

10. Due to Ireland's green rolling hills, the island is known as the Emerald Isle. One of the main reasons Ireland has such beautiful green scenery is because of all the rain the island receives throughout the year. If you want to know how much rain Ireland can get, it once rained for 40 days straight during 2007!

11. Ireland's flag as three colors and each color stands for a part of Irish culture. The color oranges stands for the people who followed William of Orange. The Gaelic tradition of Ireland is represented by the color green. The white stripe in the middle of the Irish flag stands for peace.

12. Ireland has almost 7,000 pubs on its island and claims to have the oldest pub in the world, which opened in 900 A.D and is known as Sean's Bar. Other older pubs in Ireland you can check out when you go visit include Cork City's Gateway Bar, which was established in 1698, Morahan's Roscommon, which came onto the pub scene in 1641, and Kyteler's Inn, which is located in Kilkenny opened in 1263. Of course, there are several more pubs which opened hundreds of year ago.

13. Ireland is an island, which means it's near

completely surrounded by water. In fact, Ireland is so isolated in comparison to other European areas that many of the animals found in Europe are not found in Ireland. For example, you won't be able to find weasels or moles in Ireland.

14. If you're a Bram Stoker's Dracula fan, you will want to check out Ireland because Stoker's idea for the novel is believed to have ties to Ireland. Abhartach is an Irish legend which many people believe inspired Stoker to write Dracula. The legend states that Abhartach was a jealous Irish man who believed his wife was having an affair, so he decided to spy on her. In trying to catch his wife in the act, he climbed out of a castle window but fell to his death after he slipped. The next day, Abhartach returned and started to ask people for bowls of human blood.

15. While many people see leprechauns as little men, in Irish folklore, they are actually tiny men who can stand on top of your shoulder. The Irish see leprechauns as very helpful and would never bring harm to anyone. Of course, the Irish also believe that the leprechauns know where the pot of gold is at the end of every rainbow. Furthermore, the Irish also believe that the leprechauns have also buried pots of gold throughout the island.

16. If you ever see a child's birthday in Ireland, don't be surprised if you see the child's parents bump the child's head into the birthday cake. Many Irish people believe that if a child bumps his or her head into the birthday cake, the child will see good luck throughout the year. But, in order for good luck to

come to the child, the child has to bump his or her head into the birthday cake for each year he or she has been on earth. For example, if the child is six years old, the child will bump his or her head into the cake six times.

17. One of Dublin's suburbs is called Dalkey and is known to be a neighborhood where many of Ireland's celebrities live. For example, members of the band U2 have homes in Dalkey along with Jim Sheridan, Enya, and Van Morrison.

18. Along with the show Game of Thrones, Ireland has also been the location of filming for popular movies, such as Braveheart, The Princess Bride, Harry Potter, and Star Wars. There are a lot of different filming locations to check out while you're visiting Ireland!

Bibliography

7 Famous Irish Myths and Legends. (2017). Retrieved from https://blog.expedia.ie/blog/2017/11/15/7-famous-irish-myths-legends/.

"10 Best Small Luxury Cruises To Ireland For 2019-2020 By Adventure Life". Adventure-Life.Com, https://www.adventure-life.com/ireland.

10 Great Reasons to Visit Limerick - Independent.ie. (2019). Retrieved from https://www.independent.ie/life/travel/ireland/10-great-reasons-to-visit-limerick-31147541.html.

11 Best Currency Converter Apps 2019. Retrieved from https://en.softonic.com/solutions/what-are-the-best-currency-converter-apps.

15 shocking facts you probably didn't know about Ireland!. (2019). Retrieved from https://www.irelandbeforeyoudie.com/15-facts-you-probably-didnt-know-about-ireland/.

15 of Ireland's Oldest Pubs to Discover - Irish Pubs - Expedia.ie. Retrieved from https://blog.expedia.ie/blog/2018/05/27/irelands-15-oldest-pubs-to-discover/.

17 Top Ireland Packing List Items + What to Wear & NOT To Bring (2019). Retrieved from https://www.asherfergusson.com/must-have-ireland-packing-list-items/.

20 interesting facts about Ireland. (2018). Retrieved from https://www.atlasandboots.com/interesting-facts-about-ireland/.

A local's guide to the 8 oldest pubs in Ireland - Ireland's 8 oldest pubs. Retrieved from http://tbexcon.com/blog/oldest-pubs-in-ireland/.

Abhartach The Irish Vampire - Irish Folklore & Ghost Stories From... Retrieved from https://www.yourirish.com/folklore/abhartach-irish-vampire.

About Us - The Hunt Museum. Retrieved from http://www.huntmuseum.com/about-us/.

"Airports In Ireland - Irishtourist.Com". Irishtourist.Com, http://www.irishtourist.com/travel-info/airports-in-ireland/.

Authenticireland.com. (n.d.). Weather in Ireland - Irish Weather Guide | Authentic Ireland Travel. [online] Available at: https://www.authenticireland.com/weather-in-ireland/.

Balston, Catherine. "Top 10 Foods To Try In Ireland". *BBC Good Food*, https://www.bbcgoodfood.com/howto/guide/top-10-foods-try-ireland.

Ballintoy Harbour, Ballycastle. Retrieved from https://discovernorthernireland.com/Ballintoy-Harbour-Ballintoy-Ballycastle-P11983/?s=D94AA379B90BC6BB2BC889DE5B11603E8AFB2603.

Biege, B. (2018). *The Best Time to Visit Ireland*. [online] TripSavvy. Available at:

https://www.tripsavvy.com/when-to-travel-to-ireland-1542769.

Biege, B. "There's Something To Do Every Month In Ireland". *Tripsavvy*, 2018, https://www.tripsavvy.com/ireland-month-by-month-1542583.

Biege, Bernd. "What You Need To Know About The Battle Of The Boyne". Tripsavvy, 2018, https://www.tripsavvy.com/the-battle-of-the-boyne-p2-1542488.

Biege, Bernd. "Do The Irish Celebrate Saint Martin's Day? And How?". Tripsavvy, 2017, https://www.tripsavvy.com/saint-martins-day-in-ireland-1542564.

Birbeck, A. (n.d.). 17 Top-Rated Tourist Attractions in Ireland | PlanetWare. [online] Planetware.com. Available at: https://www.planetware.com/tourist-attractions/ireland-irl.htm.

"Bloomsday Festival". Bloomsday Festival, http://www.bloomsdayfestival.ie/.

Choi, B. (n.d.). How Much Does it Cost to go to Ireland? - Money We Have. [online] Money We Have. Available at: https://www.moneywehave.com/how-much-does-it-cost-to-go-to-ireland/.

Cliffs of Moher Tour Including Wild Atlantic Way and Galway City from Dublin provided by Wild Rover Tours | Dublin, County Dublin - TripAdvisor. Retrieved from https://www.tripadvisor.com/AttractionProductReview-g186605-d11464672-

Cliffs_of_Moher_Tour_Including_Wild_Atlantic_Way_and_Galway_City_from_Dublin-Dubli.html.

Connemara Pub Tours (Galway) - 2019 All You Need to Know BEFORE You Go (with Photos) - TripAdvisor. (2019). Retrieved from https://www.tripadvisor.com/Attraction_Review-g186609-d6923070-Reviews-Connemara_Pub_Tours-Galway_County_Galway_Western_Ireland.html.

Cork Ghost Tour - 2019 All You Need to Know BEFORE You Go (with Photos) - TripAdvisor. Retrieved from https://www.tripadvisor.com/Attraction_Review-g186600-d10521685-Reviews-Cork_Ghost_Tour-Cork_County_Cork.html.

Donnellan, J. (2018). Top 5 Spectator Sports in Ireland. Retrieved from https://blog.crystal-travel.com/top-5-spectator-sports-in-ireland.

"Dublin Pass Prices". Dublinpass.Com, https://www.dublinpass.com/dublin-pass-prices.php.

Dublin Travel Guide. Retrieved from https://travel.usnews.com/Dublin_Ireland/.

Dublin Castle - TripAdvisor. (2019). Retrieved from https://www.tripadvisor.com/Attraction_Review-g186605-d214882-Reviews-Dublin_Castle-Dublin_County_Dublin.html.

Dublin Traditional Irish Music Pub Crawl provided by Traditional Irish Musical Pub Crawl | Dublin, County Dublin - TripAdvisor. (2019). Retrieved from https://www.tripadvisor.com/AttractionProductReview-g186605-d12178175-

Dublin_Traditional_Irish_Music_Pub_Crawl-Dublin_County_Dublin.html.

Earls, Richard B. "Ireland Off-Season". Travelhoppers, 2017, https://www.travelhoppers.com/articles/ireland-off-season/.

Ebert, S. What to Pack for Ireland - Tortuga Backpacks Blog. Retrieved from https://blog.tortugabackpacks.com/ireland-packing-list/.

"Galway International Arts Festival 15 - 28 July 2019 | Ireland". Giaf.Ie, https://www.giaf.ie/.

"Gaelic Games - An Introduction". Experience Gaelic Games, https://experiencegaelicgames.com/what-is-experience-gaelic-games/.

"Gaelic Games". En.Wikipedia.Org, https://en.wikipedia.org/wiki/Gaelic_games.

Game of Thrones Tours - Dublin Winterfell Trek provided by Game of Thrones Tours | Dublin, County Dublin - TripAdvisor. Retrieved from https://www.tripadvisor.com/AttractionProductReview-g186605-d15302945-Game_of_Thrones_Tours_Dublin_Winterfell_Trek-Dublin_County_Dublin.html.

GAME OF THRONES™: The Touring Exhibition, Belfast. Retrieved from https://discovernorthernireland.com/GAME-OF-THRONES-The-Touring-Exhibition-Belfast-P78087/?s=1C46D3E9DBD1FE1B279165B1082C8545748ECE8E.

Guinness Storehouse | Visit Dublin. (2019). Retrieved from https://www.visitdublin.com/see-do/details/guinness-storehouse.

"Holyhead To Dublin Ferry Tickets, Compare Times And Prices". Directferries.Co.Uk, 2019, https://www.directferries.co.uk/holyhead_dublin_ferry.htm.

"How Does The Dublin Pass Work?". Dublinpass.Com, https://www.dublinpass.com/what-you-get/how-it-works.html.

Interesting facts about Ireland. Retrieved from https://www.eupedia.com/ireland/trivia.shtml.

Ireland is the 2nd "Most Excellent" Country in the World, According to TripAdvisor. Retrieved from https://www.irelandbeforeyoudie.com/ireland-is-the-2nd-most-excellent-country-in-the-world-according-to-tripadvisor/.

Ireland - Government and society. Retrieved from https://www.britannica.com/place/Ireland/Government-and-society.

Ireland Population (2019) - Worldometers. Retrieved from http://www.worldometers.info/world-population/ireland-population/.

Ireland's weather. Retrieved from https://www.ireland.com/en-us/about-ireland/discover-ireland/irelands-weather/.

Irish Culture Facts. Retrieved from http://www.softschools.com/facts/cultures/irish_culture_facts/3256/.

Irish Currency & Money - Tourist Information Dublin. Retrieved from http://www.tourist-information-dublin.co.uk/guides/tourist-information-advice/irish-currency-money/.

Irish EU Presidency, Irish Politics, and Government: Irish Political system. Retrieved from http://eu2013.ie/ireland-and-the-presidency/about-ireland/irishpoliticsandgovernment/irishpoliticalsystem/.

Irish Fireside Travel and Culture. (2019). How Much Does a Trip to Ireland Cost?. [online] Available at: http://irishfireside.com/2014/02/05/how-much-does-a-trip-to-ireland-cost/.

"Irish History | Find Out About The History Of Ireland". *Peter Sommer Travels*, https://www.petersommer.com/ireland/history.

The Irish Pub Tour (8 - 9 Days Tour Package). Retrieved from https://www.goirishtours.com/the-irish-pub-tour/.

Ireland.com. (n.d.). *Ireland's weather*. [online] Available at: https://www.ireland.com/en-us/about-ireland/discover-ireland/irelands-weather/.

Itinerary | 8 Night Best of Ireland Tour | Self Drive Tour of Ireland. Retrieved from https://www.irishtourism.com/8-night-self-drive-tours/best-of-ireland-tour-8-night-/1662.

Logan, Hannah. "Affordable Castle Hotels In Ireland (A True Fairytale Experience) - Eat Sleep Breathe Travel". Eat Sleep Breathe Travel, 2018, https://www.eatsleepbreathetravel.com/8-affordable-castle-hotels-in-ireland/.

"Liverpool Birkenhead To Belfast Ferry | Book Tickets Online | Direct Ferries". Directferries.Co.Uk, https://www.directferries.co.uk/liverpool_birkenhead_belfast_ferry.htm.

Macardle, M. (2018). *https://www.travelandleisure.com*. [online] Travel + Leisure. Available at: https://www.travelandleisure.com/travel-tips/best-time-to-visit-ireland.

Malahide Castle - 2019 All You Need to Know BEFORE You Go (with Photos) - TripAdvisor. (2019). Retrieved from https://www.tripadvisor.com/Attraction_Review-g211873-d216166-Reviews-Malahide_Castle-Malahide_County_Dublin.html.

Money in Ireland. Retrieved from https://www.ireland.com/en-us/about-ireland/must-know-information/money-in-ireland/.

Maloney, L. (2018). The Best Way to Travel to Ireland. [online] Traveltips.usatoday.com. Available at: https://traveltips.usatoday.com/way-travel-ireland-31067.html.

Middleton, J. (n.d.). *Why Visit Ireland? 10 Essential Experiences on the Emerald Isle*. [online] Reader's Digest. Available at: https://www.readersdigest.ca/travel/world/10-magical-reasons-visit-ireland/.

Muckross-house.ie. (n.d.). Muckross House Killarney�Gardens of Ireland � Killarney Attractions - Killarney National Park �Muckross Park. [online] Available at: http://www.muckross-house.ie/house-garden.html.

"National Ploughing Championships". Npa.Ie, http://www.npa.ie/.

"Roscoff To Cork Ferry Tickets, Compare Times And Prices". Directferries.Co.Uk, https://www.directferries.co.uk/roscoff_cork_ferry.htm.

The President | President of Ireland. Retrieved from https://president.ie/en/the-president/constitutional-role.

Top Currency Calculators for International Travel. Retrieved from https://www.tripsavvy.com/top-currency-calculators-3150158.

Rareirishstuff.com. (n.d.). *History of Ireland.* [online] Available at: https://www.rareirishstuff.com/about-us/about-you.406.html.

Retrieved from http://nationfacts.net/ireland-facts/.

Ring of Kerry Tourism Co Kerry Ireland. (2019). Retrieved from https://ringofkerrytourism.com/.

Ross Castle (Killarney) - 2019 All You Need to Know BEFORE You Go (with Photos) - TripAdvisor. (2019). Retrieved from https://www.tripadvisor.com/Attraction_Review-g186612-d215124-Reviews-Ross_Castle-Killarney_County_Kerry.html.

Rural Pub Tours (Dublin) - 2019 All You Need to Know BEFORE You Go (with Photos) - TripAdvisor. (2019). Retrieved from https://www.tripadvisor.com/Attraction_Review-g186605-d1412909-Reviews-Rural_Pub_Tours-Dublin_County_Dublin.html.

Ten Irish Cultural Traditions And Their Origins. Retrieved from https://www.irelandbeforeyoudie.com/ten-origins-irish-cultural-traditions/.

"The 10 Most Famous Irish Myths And Legends Of All-Time". *Ireland Before You Die*, https://www.irelandbeforeyoudie.com/the-10-most-famous-myths-and-legends-from-irish-folklore/.

"Top 7 Irish Festivals 2019". *Ireland Tours - Small Group Vacation Tours Around Ireland*, 2018, https://vagabondtoursofireland.com/top-irish-festivals-2019/.

The 148th Open, Royal Portrush, Portrush. Retrieved from https://discovernorthernireland.com/The-148th-Open-Royal-Portrush-Portrush-P63861/.

The Aran Islands - Galway Ireland - Aran Islands - Galway - Doolin. Retrieved from http://www.aranislands.ie/.

The Glens of Antrim. Retrieved from https://discovernorthernireland.com/about-northern-ireland/destinations/causeway/the-glens-of-antrim/?s=B5694A65614FAFB9A7AF29076A9EE53A312EF0B3.

Trim Castle - 2019 All You Need to Know BEFORE You Go (with Photos) - TripAdvisor. Retrieved from https://www.tripadvisor.com/Attraction_Review-g644237-d525404-Reviews-Trim_Castle-Trim_County_Meath.html.

"Santander To Cork Ferry Tickets, Compare Times And Prices". Directferries.Co.Uk, https://www.directferries.co.uk/santander_cork_ferry.htm.

"Wexford Festival Opera 2019". Wexford Festival Opera 2019, https://www.wexfordopera.com/.

"What Is The Dublin Pass And What Do You Get?". Dublinpass.Com, https://www.dublinpass.com/what-you-get/.